GHOSTS OF

GHOSTS
OF
ESSEX

Betty Puttick

COUNTRYSIDE BOOKS
NEWBURY, BERKSHIRE

First published 1997
© Betty Puttick 1997

Countryside Books
3 Catherine Road
Newbury, Berkshire

ISBN 1 85306 465 3

Cover illustration by Colin Doggett

Produced through MRM Associates Ltd., Reading
Typeset by Acorn Bookwork, Salisbury
Printed by J. W. Arrowsmith Ltd., Bristol

Contents

Ghosts
of
Essex

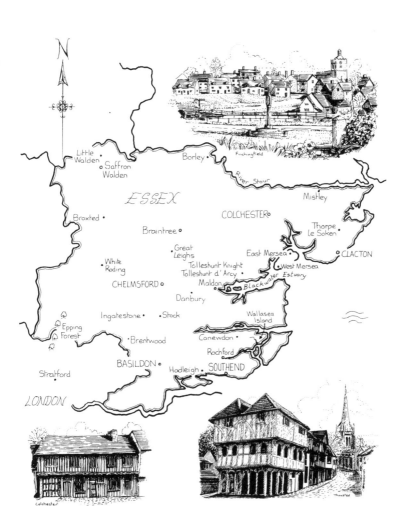

N

Little
Walden
Saffron
Walden

Borley

Finchingfield

River Stour

Mistley

ESSEX

Broxted

COLCHESTER

Thorpe
Le Soken

Braintree

CLACTON

Great
Leighs

East Mersea

White
Roding

Tolleshunt Knight
Tolleshunt d'Arcy

West Mersea

Blackwater Estuary

CHELMSFORD

Maldon

Danbury

Ingatestone

Stock

Wallasea
Island

Epping
Forest

Brentwood

Canewdon

Rochford

BASILDON

Stratford

Hadleigh

SOUTHEND

LONDON

Colchester

Thaxted

Acknowledgements

My grateful thanks to all the people who took the time and trouble to help me with my enquiries, especially Tom Hodgson, Jacqueline McEwan and Dawn Moor, and my good friend, Wesley H. Downes, Area Officer for the Eastern Region of the Ghost Club Society. What Wesley does not know about Essex ghosts is not worth knowing, and his generous help is much appreciated.

Introduction

WHEN James Wentworth Day wrote, not so long ago, 'This old land of the Danes, asleep by day, is alive and awake beneath the moon at night' he caught the strange, mysterious character of his home county, Essex.

I have had books published about the ghosts of three counties, Hertfordshire, Buckinghamshire and Bedfordshire, each with its own crop of strange stories and uncanny happenings – but Essex is something else. It almost seems like two counties, one consisting of the large, busy towns and the other the quiet places, once isolated and remote, where the belief in ghosts, witches and the Devil flourished and where even today stories of spectral Romans and Vikings abroad on Mersea Island and Canvey Point do not seem so unlikely, especially on a dark night when the wind howls across the marshes and trees and shadows assume strange shapes.

Essex is called 'The Witch County' with good reason. From his base at Mistley, evil Matthew Hopkins, the Witch-finder General, carried out his relentless vendetta against those accused of consorting with the Devil and was responsible for the deaths of hundreds of women. Small wonder that his ghost is restless.

Stories of witch ghosts, too, persist and Hallowe'en sees hopeful crowds gather at Canewdon church where one of the best known usually disappoints her public by refusing to appear to order...

But there is no shortage of ghosts in Essex. Inns, council offices, a railway station, a disused airfield, a museum, a farm, Epping Forest and of course famous Borley, all have their stories of the supernatural. And, on a lighter note, there are encounters with the Little Folk who still appear in Essex for those with eyes to see them.

Everyone likes a good ghost story, especially if it is true, and interest in the paranormal has never been stronger. Over the years I have had my own encounters with the supernatural and I find that wherever I go I meet people who have also had strange experiences hard to explain in everyday terms.

Wherever possible I visit the haunted sites I write about, and talk to those involved, as there is often something new or unexpected to discover. There is all the difference in the world between an old ghostly legend and yesterday's eye witness account, but it is all fascinating and no easier to explain than it has ever been.

The ghosts of Essex are more mysterious than most. I hope you will enjoy meeting them in my book.

Betty Puttick

Portrait of a Ghost?

COLCHESTER'S Hollytrees Museum of dolls, toys, costume and so on is housed in a fine Georgian building in the town. If you climb the stairs to the second floor, you will find the portrait of a charmingly dressed lady, Miss Anne Lisle, said to be the sister of an eminent apothecary of the town. From the style of her dress, hair and bonnet, she belongs possibly to the 18th century, but to the visitor her dark eyes seem alive and her pale, rather severe face is not friendly.

Not long ago a teenage girl was looking at the portrait when she heard footsteps behind her. This was a little odd as the floor is carpeted and would usually mask the sound, and when she looked round there was no one about at all. And yet she could still hear footsteps passing through the room, and down the stairs to the entrance hall.

She was still standing in front of the portrait when shortly afterwards she was startled to see a ghostly figure rush past her into the Gun Room. Looking as frightened as she felt she hurried down the stairs, and as she passed the attendant's desk he said, 'Don't worry, you're not the only one who's seen it.'

True enough, there have been a number of times when visitors have encountered something strange in the museum. Small children, taken to see the dolls and toys, seem to be especially sensitive to the atmosphere. One little girl in the Gun Room complained that she did not like the lady standing next to her Daddy, but as far as her father and the museum assistant were concerned, there was no one there. And other children insist on going away as they say 'someone is there' and feel afraid.

Footsteps have often been heard by attendants at a time when there are no visitors in the building, a sound quite distinct from the creaking of old floorboards. A former assistant described what he had heard as rapid footsteps 'like a lady'. He said that various people have sensed something odd and mentioned two ladies who hurried downstairs because they felt a presence in the Gun Room. And another visitor said she heard a piano playing, although there is no piano in the museum.

One day the same man called two other assistants who were working upstairs to come down for a cup of tea. He didn't take much notice as two people came downstairs and one turned down the corridor to the kitchen. But soon afterwards the second assistant came down the stairs on his own! So who was the third figure who had gone towards the kitchen and disappeared without trace?

Close to Hollytrees Museum is East Lodge, once two houses and now used by Colchester Borough Council as offices. From time to time an apparition they call the White Lady has been seen on the stairs, or flitting from room to room, pausing sometimes to watch the staff at work.

A builder busy plastering the kitchen had an unnerving experience one day. He sensed that someone had come in behind him, and assumed it was his labourer, but when he spoke to him, and received no reply, he looked round. The White Lady was standing there in the doorway, and as he stared the figure just faded away. The builder threw down his tools and ran outside in a state of shock, and was off work for some time afterwards.

The best eye witness account of the ghost, however, comes from an East Lodge cleaning lady, who insists that what happened is strictly true.

She was alone in the building, having said goodnight to the office workers as they went home, and was busy with her usual work. She was cleaning a mark on the carpet in a room where the original two houses meet and an entrance has been made in the central wall between the two rooms. She became aware of slight noises, like scratching and rustling, and then the unmistakable sound of computer keys being tapped in the adjoining room. She knew no one had come in, and she had seen everyone leave, so what could it be?

'I walked slowly towards the room, wishing I was anywhere else but there,' she said. There was a faint smell of perfume which gradually became stronger and she was conscious of a presence although the room seemed to be empty. She knew the room had been perfectly tidy when she left it but now pens were scattered all over the floor. The palms of her hands were damp and she tried to ignore the scared feeling that was growing within her.

'But as I turned to walk out of the room, there she stood,' she went on. 'She was of small stature, her crinoline gown and bonnet were grey, and she wore fingerless lace gloves on her hands. She was there one minute and then gone.'

Thinking it over at home later, she asked herself if it had really happened, but every detail of the ghostly apparition was imprinted clearly on her memory, the scent of her perfume, and especially the strange fact that the White Lady had no face!

This was just one of the happenings over the years such as lights going on and off, doors closing by themselves, chairs moving when no one was nearby and desk drawers opening and closing. The staff are used to it and just say 'Oh dear, she's at it again.'

So who is the White Lady? The cleaning lady's description does bear quite a resemblance to Miss Anne Lisle as she appears in her portrait in Hollytrees Museum. And consider one other point – one morning when they opened the Gun Room at Hollytrees there was an overpowering scent of perfume that lasted for two days. And when the cleaning lady had her encounter with the ghost at East

Lodge a smell of perfume was the first thing she noticed!

So do the two buildings share a ghost? I understand that Miss Lisle and her brother did not live at Hollytrees and do not appear to have had connections with East Lodge, so the mystery remains. Does she accompany her portrait, or is the ghost someone else entirely? Shall we ever know?

There is something particularly eerie about ghosts that have a curious attachment to their own pictures. If you visit Bisham Abbey in Berkshire, for example, now the National Sports Centre, you will see the full-length portrait of Dame Elizabeth Hoby whose home it once was. For centuries her restless spirit has roamed the old Abbey by the river grieving for the young son she is said to have killed in a fury over his smudged and blotted copy books.

She looks a formidable lady, her icily imperious face and long, tapering hands white against her black gown. The strange aspect of Dame Hoby's haunting is that she appears to step out of the picture, leaving the frame empty, and her ghost is seen in the negative, that is her huge floating white headdress, ruff and frilled sleeves appear black, and her black gown white.

She drifts through the Abbey, a bowl floating in front of her, and, like a grief-stricken Lady Macbeth, she repeatedly washes her hands, trying to remove the traces of her guilt.

Miss Henrietta Nelson is another lady whose portrait shows a sad, unsmiling face beneath her ornate 18th-century hat. She led an unhappy life at Yaxley Hall, near Eye, Suffolk, treated unkindly by her family because she was illegitimate. She died after a fall in 1815 and was buried in a mausoleum in the grounds, but later, after her coffin was moved, Henrietta began to haunt and wherever her portrait went thereafter, her ghost followed.

The picture was bought around 1950 by a collector, Bryan Hall, who soon discovered that Henrietta was now haunting his home and grounds at Banningham Rectory, Norfolk. But in 1995 her portrait was among a hoard of valuable antiques stolen from the house and Mr Hall was convinced that Henrietta's spirit had gone too.

I wonder what would happen to Colchester's White Lady if Miss Ann Lisle's portrait were ever moved?

The Most Hated Man in East Anglia

D URING the 1970s a journalist, Russell Edwards, reported that while on a visit to Mistley he had taken a photograph of the ancient Thorn Inn. To his surprise, when his film was developed it showed a mysterious ghostly figure standing outside. As far as he knew, there had been no one, supernatural or otherwise, present when he took his picture, so who could it have been?

As many inhabitants of the neighbourhood could have told him, one name immediately comes to mind. Matthew Hopkins, the self-styled Witchfinder General, whose deadly reign of terror during the 17th century has never been forgotten, had his headquarters at the Thorn Inn. With a career like his, it would not be unexpected if his spirit remained earthbound and despite the 350 odd years since his death there have been many reported sightings to suggest that the ghost of Hopkins is still restless.

The son of a Puritan minister in Great Wenham, Suffolk, Hopkins claimed to have practised as a lawyer in Ipswich, although he was most probably a clerk to a shipping firm. But it was after his arrival in Manningtree that he found the career for which he became notorious. Witchcraft has a long, dark history but after the passing of the Witchcraft Act of 1604, the persecution of witches became an obsession and Essex in particular was known as The Witch County.

By his own account, in March 1644 Hopkins discovered 'some seven or eight of that horrible sect of witches' living

16

in his neighbourhood, who met every six weeks on Friday nights, when they 'had their several solemn sacrifices offered to the Devil'. He also reported that four of them sent the Devil in the form of a bear to kill him in his own garden, but he obviously survived unhurt to start his dedicated career of witch persecution beginning with the same four women. They were among nineteen found guilty and hanged after Chelmsford Assizes in July 1645.

Matthew Hopkins had found his forte in the hysterical days of witchcraft mania and with his side-kick John Stearne and his 'searcher', Mary Phillips, he pursued his witch-finding crusade throughout Essex, Suffolk, Norfolk, Bedfordshire and Huntingdonshire. For many people the fear of witchcraft must have been equalled by the very real fear of being falsely accused of being a witch on the slenderest of evidence. In isolated communities almost any misfortune or ailment was attributed to witchcraft by the ignorant and superstitious and some came to trial on the word of only one person, sometimes inspired by enmity or malevolence, and even children were known to accuse members of their own family.

Hopkins' self-chosen title of Witchfinder General seems to have been accepted without question, also his contention that he possessed 'the Devil's own list' of every witch in the country.

He terrorised and tortured his victims into confession, depriving them of sleep or rest for long periods, after which they were walked rapidly up and down endlessly by relays of helpers. They were often bound cross-legged to a stool with their left thumb tied to their right big toe, and their right thumb tied to their left big toe, and kept like this without food or water for days.

Mary Phillips' role was to strip search for so-called witch marks, and old scars, warts or moles often qualified as signs that the victim was in thrall to the Devil.

Not surprisingly many of Matthew Hopkins' victims,

starving and their spirit broken, gave way under such torture and confessed themselves guilty of witchcraft. Others readily admitted consorting with the Devil and would describe sending their imps or familiars to perform all kinds of wickedness on their behalf. These creatures might be dogs, cats, toads or mice with such strange names as Suckin, Vinegar Tom, Jamara and Greedigut, and Hopkins declared that their names alone could not have been invented by mortals, which gave weight to his evidence that the owner of such animals was a dabbler in the black arts.

Failing all else, suspected witches were subjected to the swimming test where, tied hand and foot, they were cast into a pond or river to sink or swim. If they floated this was taken as a sure sign that they were a witch, and if they sank they were declared innocent, which was small consolation as they usually drowned.

It was a lucrative career for Hopkins, who was well paid for his efforts, and during 1644 to 1646 he was responsible for the deaths of hundreds of women. But growing hostility at the brutality of his methods inspired John Gaule, a Huntingdonshire vicar, to publish a pamphlet in April 1646 against Hopkins' ruthless reign of terror. Eventually feeling ran so high that Hopkins published a booklet in his defence called *The Discovery of Witches* in an attempt to justify the fortune he was making out of so much human misery. But 1646 saw the end of his vendetta when he thought it prudent to retire and he died not long afterwards.

The parish records say that Matthew Hopkins was buried on the 12th August 1647 at Mistley Heath, but the manner of his death is open to doubt. One story has it that in retribution for his cruel swimming tests, Hopkins himself was set upon one day and 'swum' in the same manner, and the effect upon his health was fatal. This could tie in with another belief that he died of consumption or inflammation of the lungs, which could have been brought on by his ducking.

Yet another theory is that he survived his involuntary swim and emigrated to New England to join his brother, and maybe surfaced in another Essex, in Massachusetts, at the time of the Salem witch trials years later.

It seems incredible that one man could wreak so much evil in only two years. I visited Colchester Castle, now a museum, while writing this book and saw the room where Hopkins interrogated some of his victims. Shadows and recorded voices are used to give an alarmingly atmospheric impression of what it must have been like for those frightened women who fell into the pitiless clutches of that evil man. I happened to have walked in ahead of the next batch of visitors and as I stood alone within those crumbling walls in the half dark I could almost smell the fear of those who found themselves helplessly at the mercy of Hopkins' venomous interrogation, knowing that their only escape was at the end of a rope. It was all too much and I had to leave.

Hopkins used the Red Lion and White Hart pubs in Manningtree and the Thorn Inn at Mistley to meet informants and interrogate suspects and his ghost is known to have haunted all three places over the years. On one occasion a member of the staff at the Thorn Inn found the figure of Matthew Hopkins sitting in a chair in the attic and as he watched it got up and walked away.

Many locals fishing in the lake in the grounds of Mistley Place have encountered a ghostly figure there during recent years. It appears to resemble a shortish man, only about five foot tall, wearing old style clothes, knee boots and a tall hat, a description which fits Matthew Hopkins.

Two young fishermen were there one night when they saw the figure clearly in the moonlight, only about ten feet away from them. It stood quite still for a time and then began to drift closer, at which one of them swung his rod round towards it. It passed right through the figure and, terrified, they dropped their gear and ran away as fast as they could.

Along The Walls at Mistley there is a small hump-backed bridge known as the Hopping Bridge, and there have been many reports of apparitions in the vicinity. Sometimes it is a phantom jaywalker, apt to step out into the road to the alarm of any passing motorist but when the driver brakes hastily and draws up the mysterious pedestrian is nowhere to be seen.

In the early 1960s, one man walking by the bridge saw a similar apparition run across the road towards Mistley Place and vanish. He told the *Harwich and Manningtree Standard* that the figure appeared to be wearing 17th-century clothes and that he was convinced he had seen the ghost of Matthew Hopkins. Mistley Place is one of the sites where Hopkins' body may have been buried and when the man returned next day to examine the place where the ghost disappeared he found a patch of thicker, darker grass 'about six foot by three, like there might be a grave underneath'.

A clairvoyant from the Spiritualist Circle in Mistley held a seance at the Red Lion in Manningtree some time ago at which Hopkins apparently put in an appearance. 'I just suddenly saw him', she said, 'wearing dark clothing, no hat, holding a cane, dank oily hair, dark, glittering eyes, and small beard and moustache. He stared at me and then disappeared. He seemed to be of the sixteenth or seventeenth century and I did not realise who he was until afterwards.'

A footnote to Hopkins' reign of terror was provided on 9th May 1921 when a man digging in his garden at St Osyth uncovered the skeletons of two women. They were buried with their heads to the north which indicated that they were executed witches who were traditionally buried in this manner in unconsecrated ground. Their bones were riveted by iron spikes, elbow to elbow, wrist to wrist, knee to knee and ankle to ankle, in an extraordinary manner and it was recalled that in the days of the witch hunts it was the custom to secure a witch's body so that she could never rise again from her grave and haunt her neighbours. The skeletons were thought to have been about 300 years old, and may well have been those of two of Matthew Hopkins' victims.

Despite Hopkins' efforts, witchcraft continued to flourish in some parts of Essex where the black art found another powerful opponent in the form of Cunning Murrell whose familiar boast 'I am the Devil's Master' struck fear into many a heart. But that is another story.

Ghosts Galore

Ghosts, in Essex as elsewhere, can have diverse character-istics . . . .

Helpful Ghosts

STATELY homes and manor houses can usually boast a stately ghost or two, perhaps an aristocratic lady or a knight with a suitably historic pedigree. But others find that their particular apparition may come from below stairs, and rather than drifting aimlessly along the battlements or causing cold draughts in the great hall, ghostly servants have sometimes been known to make themselves useful.

The Manor House at Weeley has long enjoyed the services of a very helpful ghost. One past resident was surprised and pleased to find that while he was out his room had been mysteriously tidied up. And, even more amazing, once a complete dinner service was moved from the kitchen dresser, cleaned and returned. And, not content with this, the ghostly housekeeper gave the whole kitchen a good spring clean!

Some occupants of the Manor House were conscious of a presence and others more sensitive actually glimpsed an elderly lady who apparently had a habit of losing her old-fashioned hairpins which were scattered all over the house. At times various items would disappear and turn up elsewhere, but most residents were happy with their ghostly home help's little ways.

A Hospital Haunt

THE Essex County Hospital at Colchester seems an unlikely place for a ghost story, especially in the children's ward, but a local man has never forgotten what happened when he was a patient there as a child.

He was in bed there one night when he saw a nun in a black habit coming towards him. She spoke kindly to him and gave him a toffee from a brown paper bag she was carrying. Surprised, he popped it in his mouth and watched as she walked on down the ward and he couldn't believe it when she then just disappeared in front of his eyes.

Father William's Return

FATHER William was a remarkable old Essex character and several stories about him can be found in S.L. Bensusan's books on the county.

Bensusan lived near the mouth of the Blackwater Estuary and Father William inhabited a small thatched cottage next door which had been his home for nearly ninety years. But while Bensusan was away from home some well-meaning people, thinking that the old man could no longer look after himself properly at his age, removed him to the local workhouse despite his protests.

When Bensusan returned home he was horrified to find out what had happened to his old friend, and even more horrified on arriving at the workhouse to discover that Father William had died. The workhouse master, obviously at a loss to explain the old man's fate said, 'I can't understand it. The old chap was living all alone, scratching for himself, uncared for and probably not one square meal a day, and here he pines away and dies.'

'So would a wild bird if you put it in a cage,' replied Bensusan.

An elderly widow moved into the old man's cottage,

but shortly afterwards she came to see Bensusan in a state of alarm. When she went into the sitting room she had found the ghost of Father William sitting in an armchair in front of the fireplace, just as he used to do. And for a few nights afterwards he was there in his old chair, returned in spirit to the home he loved.

The Haunted Homecare Shop

IN the late fifties and early sixties many an old cinema fell on hard times, and this was the fate of Clacton's old Kinema. Even while it was in use there were rumours that it was haunted and this was thought to be connected with the suicide of a projectionist who had been overwhelmed with grief when his son was killed during the war.

After the cinema closed it stayed empty for a time, then the building was reconstructed and became a shop that was ultimately taken over by a well-known wallpaper and paint business. Then in the late eighties a young girl working there had a frightening experience. She had gone up to the store room on the top floor but came running back down the stairs and said she had seen an old man up there.

As she described him he sounded like a figure from one of the old gangster movies which must often have been on the programme at the old Kinema. With his sleek, brilliantined hair and pinstriped suit, this George Raft look-alike took no notice of her at all, and the young girl assistant, in a state of shock, had turned and run.

There were other sightings of the same figure, and two other assistants were standing together in one of the upper rooms one day when they both felt a hand placed on their shoulders, and as they turned to look they were roughly flung aside by a misty shape which rushed towards the wall and disappeared.

A young male assistant was sent upstairs on another occasion to get a particular roll of wallpaper from the stock room and as he looked around for it he could hear someone coming up the stairs. Thinking it was the manager he called out, but when there was no reply he went to the top of the stairs. To his amazement there was no one in sight and yet the footsteps continued up the stairs towards him, passed by and went on towards a staff room where the door was open. Stranger still, the footsteps turned into the staff room and the door then closed with a bang!

And another time when the same young man was upstairs, all the doors to the various rooms up there began to slam backwards and forwards at the same time.

The shop was refitted in 1993 and two workmen from a London firm decided to save money by camping out in one of the upper rooms instead of taking lodgings. However, after one night they changed their minds as they didn't get a wink of sleep due to the heavy-footed ghost stomping about all night long!

Punctual Ghosts

THERE are ghosts who appear regular as clockwork on a certain date and Sir John Gates is one of these. Beeleigh Abbey at Maldon was once his home which he is said to have bought for £300 in 1537, and although he held various high positions, including High Sheriff of Essex in 1549, he unfortunately became involved in the plot to put Lady Jane Grey on the throne, and paid the price on Tower Hill where he was beheaded on 22nd August 1553.

Beeleigh Abbey had by that time passed into other hands but the 'haunting wailing around the house' on August 11th each year is believed to be Sir John's cries of misery at his imminent execution. On the actual anniversary of his death his headless apparition has been seen in the James Room.

This particular room has a history of strange happenings, and people in there have had the sensation of being watched. On one occasion a housekeeper saw a hooded figure there, which may have been a monk. The Abbey was a monastery for monks of the Cistercian Order in the 12th century and was partly destroyed under the Dissolution of the Monasteries Acts in Henry VIII's time.

Curious about the happenings in the James Room, one of the Abbey's owners decided one night to sleep there for the first time, but it proved to be an unforgettable experience. She woke at about 3 am to find that the heavy four poster bed on which she lay was shaking violently and, in fact, everything in the room seemed to be shaking too in an alarming manner.

In addition, she found that her arm felt very painful and swollen as a result of what seemed to be a large bite. She visited the hospital next morning and although the doctor said it certainly was not a mosquito bite, he was at a loss to identify it as it seemed more like the bite of a tropical creature of some kind.

Well, ghosts don't bite, do they, so what attacked the Abbey's owner that night in the haunted James Room? The lovely old Abbey is obviously a place of many strange secrets. And here's another. A few years ago when there was a lengthy drought and a consequent shortage of water in rivers and ponds, it seemed a good time to clear out the Abbey pond. And down in the mud and silt a grisly heap of human skeletons was uncovered! At some period during the Abbey's long history they must have been deposited there, but why? And who were they? It seems hardly surprising that poor Sir John Gates is not Beeleigh Abbey's only ghost!

Freddie the Theatre Royal Phantom

SEVERAL London Boroughs were once part of Essex, like Stratford where the old Theatre Royal is best known as the home of Joan Littlewood's Theatre Workshop.

When Joan and her company moved into the theatre it was in a sleazy and run-down condition and under threat of possible demolition, but their arrival brought new life to the old building in Angel Lane. This must have pleased the resident ghost, Freddie Fredericks, who built the theatre in 1880 and has been keeping a careful eye on it ever since.

Many of the Theatre Workshop actors suffered from their profession's customary problem, shortage of money, and often camped out in the dressing rooms, as did the self-appointed, unpaid caretaker, George Cooper, who had established himself in the boiler room, although he did have a home in nearby Skiers Road.

George lived a frugal life and managed to save some of the tips people gave him which he safely stashed away in an old tin box. By the time he died in 1968, rumour was that George had collected a small fortune in his battered old treasure chest, which was hidden somewhere in the theatre. George believed that his money would never be found by the wrong person as the ghost of Freddie Fredericks was looking after it for him.

'The money is in a tin box and there is a book saying who to give it to' were his last words on the subject, presumably addressed to Freddie, but what happened after that is Freddie's secret!

A former manager of the theatre, Gerry Raffles, described Freddie as 'a small tubby fellow, dressed in brown. I have often been very conscious of his presence late at night, about midnight. But he is obviously a friendly ghost, of whom there's no need to be afraid. He is part of the building after all ... Mr Fredericks was at the theatre in the early days when it was very successful. Then the Borough Theatre was built in Stratford High Street and took the gilt away.'

During a production of *The Invisible Man* in 1992, the leading actor, Michael Harbour, had made a quick costume change during the performance and was hurrying back on stage when a man in a light-coloured suit appeared to walk towards him out of the scenery props. The figure was also seen by the actor's dresser, and was assumed to be Freddie.

I have seen a photograph of Freddie, whose real name was Albert and who lived from 1840 to 1901. He had a splendid moustache and neat imperial beard, and wore pince-nez. The tradition at the Theatre Royal is that he appears nightly to make sure that his initials 'F.F.' remain in the centre of the proscenium arch over the stage, and it is said that if they are ever painted over or removed, the theatre will fall down!

The Strange Story of Borley

A GROUP of us sat intently listening to a tape recording one evening recently. At first there was nothing, followed by a few raps and scratches, and then it came. It was a noise that looking back I find almost indescribable, a harsh, menacing cry that might have come from the throat of some primeval beast. It was enough to chill the blood and we looked at each other, stunned into silence by the sheer evil of it.

The tape had been made by leaving a 'bug' one morning inside Borley church. Many recordings have been made there and have produced a variety of sounds such as doors opening and closing, bolts being withdrawn, footsteps, knocking or tapping, even snatches of organ music while the church is known to be empty.

I cannot give any explanation for what was captured on that tape, I only know that I cannot imagine a more terrifying sound. But this is just one of the innumerable happenings over the years that have earned Borley, in the far north-east of the county, its reputation as an extraordinary focus of paranormal activity.

Borley Rectory, destroyed by fire in 1939, is usually referred to as 'the most haunted house in England', and this is the title of a book about Borley by the psychic investigator Harry Price. As he himself explained, it was not he who invented the name. On his first visit to the area, in June 1929, when he asked a local bystander for directions to

Borley Rectory the reply was 'Oh, you mean the most haunted house in England'. Little did he imagine as he arrived at the red brick monstrosity that he would be concerned with its mysterious range of phenomena for the rest of his life.

So much has been written about Borley that I hesitated to add to it, and yet no book about the ghosts of Essex would be complete without reference to this most famous of haunted places.

Henry D.E. Bull, the then Rector of Borley, built the rectory in 1863 on the site of an older building. But local tradition says that there was a monastery there before that, and a lay brother from the monastery and a novice from the nunnery at Bures fell in love. They eloped one night in a black coach drawn by a pair of bay horses, but were captured and suffered a terrible fate. The man was hanged and the nun was bricked up alive at her own convent.

Harry Price thought there was no evidence for this story but, as he said, 'We can dismiss the legends about the nun but we cannot dismiss the lady herself'. The ghost of a nun has appeared in the grounds countless times, and there have been many sightings of a coach.

The Rev Henry Bull and his large family of fourteen children soon realised that their new home was already a much haunted house. A path alongside the lawn became known as the Nun's Walk, for obvious reasons, and the Rev Bull erected a summer house with a clear view of this path where he and his son Harry liked to sit, companionably smoking their pipes, as they waited for their apparition to appear. However, her habit of gazing at them all through the dining room window at mealtimes distressed the family, and the Rector had the main dining room window bricked up.

The nun was no midnight ghost, she frequently abroad in daylight, and one afternoon some of the Rev Bull's daughters had a close encounter. It was 28th July

1900 when Ethel, Freda and Mabel returned from a garden party and saw the nun gliding along the Nun's Walk. Freda ran indoors to fetch a fourth sister, Elsie, who, apparently thinking the figure was human, went forward to speak to it, whereupon it vanished.

The Bull family experienced other supernatural manifestations of a kind that would reach a crescendo in later years. After Henry Bull's death in 1892, his son Harry became Rector until he too died, in 1927. Harry had promised to make his own presence known after death by 'throwing moth balls about so you will know it is me' and this did indeed happen, and there have been other sightings of a tall, bearded figure resembling Harry.

Finding a new rector proved difficult and the Rev G. Eric Smith and his wife did not stay long after they moved into the rambling, inconvenient rectory in 1928. But their stay was full of incident. The nun and also the phantom coach were seen, strange lights appeared in unused rooms, bells rang, mysterious footsteps and whispering voices were heard and one morning Mrs Smith found a brown paper parcel in a cupboard. It contained a small female skull in perfect condition, its presence a complete mystery, and this was later given burial in the churchyard.

As the phenomena continued the Rev Smith appealed to the *Daily Mirror* for help, and the Editor contacted Harry Price, who went down on 12th June 1929 on the first of many visits.

The Smiths were followed at the rectory by the Rev Lionel Foyster and his wife Marianne in 1930, the signal for the psychic phenomena to escalate. A taste of what was ahead came on the very day the Foysters moved in when they heard strange footsteps moving about the house and a voice called out 'Marianne dear'.

Harry Price subsequently estimated that at least 2,000 poltergeist phenomena were experienced at the rectory between October 1930 and October 1935 while the

Foysters lived there, and the Rev Foyster kept a diary recording all that happened.

Marianne Foyster was herself psychic and seemed to be a focus for many of the happenings. She began to encounter the ghost of Harry Bull, usually on the stairs, but no one else saw him. All kinds of things went missing and reappeared elsewhere, and sometimes items arrived that did not belong to the family. Disconnected bells often rang and unexplained scents and smells permeated the house. Gradually, whatever entity was behind the activity became more vicious and things flew about, sometimes striking Marianne, and objects appeared just inside doors so that anyone entering would trip up.

The Rector obtained some holy water and performed an exorcism, to little effect as the poltergeists threw a large stone at him, and books were later pulled off the shelves and pictures taken down and thrown about. That night it was bedlam in their room as things whizzed around and on subsequent days stones and various heavy objects were thrown at the Foysters.

Messages started appearing on the walls and scraps of paper urging 'Marianne, help' and asking for 'Light', 'Mass', 'Prayers' and 'Incense'.

After the Foysters left Borley Rectory Harry Price rented the property for a year and recruited a team of volunteers to report on the happenings. His principal investigator was Sidney Glanville who with friends tried using a planchette in October 1937 to contact entities at the rectory. They received information from it that said the nun was buried in the garden under a stone.

Mr Glanville's daughter Helen tried her own experiments with a planchette at home and writing was produced giving the nun's name as Mary, or Marie, Lairre, of French nationality, who was from a nunnery at Le Havre, but was once at Bures. She hinted that she had been killed on 17 May 1667, and asked for Mass and prayers. At a subsequent seance, her age was given as 19 when she died. She said that 'Waldegrave' had taken her away from Bures, and that she was strangled in 1667. The Waldegraves, whose tomb is in Borley church, were the owners of Borley for centuries. The message ended with another request for a Requiem Mass, incense and a Christian burial.

At the end of December 1938 Captain W.H. Gregson bought the rectory and renamed it The Priory, but his time there was short. On the night of 27th February 1939 the Captain was sorting some books in the hall when a stack of them unexpectedly toppled, knocking over a paraffin lamp with dire results. The oil from the lamp caught fire and while Captain Gregson phoned the fire brigade, the flames spread rapidly. By the time the fire was extinguished the building was in ruins, and spectators claimed that during the blaze two figures had been seen at the upper windows, one a young girl. Others said that a grey clad nun had been seen slipping away from the inferno.

In 1943 Harry Price and his helpers excavated the cellar of the rectory and eventually unearthed part of a human skull and a jawbone. Were they the remains of Marie Lairre? If so, her repeated requests for Christian burial were satisfied on 29th May 1945 when Harry Price, the Rev A.C. Henning and his wife and son attended the interment of a small casket containing the remains in Liston church-yard.

The ruins of the haunted rectory are long gone and the site has been built on, but stories still surface of odd happenings in and around the church. The most macabre is the movement of the stone coffins in the crypt, often found out of place and in odd positions.

In the 1980s a couple and their daughter visited the church and, as they approached the entrance, could hear the organ playing Handel's *Largo*. But as they entered the music stopped and they were surprised to find the church empty and the organ closed. They were even more surprised when a shower of small stones fell on them from above, and they departed hurriedly.

Sightings of a nun continue to be reported and one particularly interesting event happened in June 1970. A member of a psychic investigation group was walking down the Nun's Walk at 1.45 am when in the clear moonlight he saw a nun coming towards him. As she drew nearer she moved suddenly into a hedge and the man used his walkie-talkie to summon a colleague.

As his friend appeared at the other end of the Nun's Walk, the nun re-emerged from the hedge at a place between the two men, who could both see the figure clearly. At one point she was within six feet of them, and as she stood still for a few seconds they saw that she had the face of an older woman, with a mole on her left cheek and a sad expression. Appearing oblivious of the watching men, she passed through the hedge again and vanished at the bottom of a bungalow garden.

It is curious to note that descriptions of the ghostly nun vary, some reporting a 'veiled girl' and others, as in this case, a much older woman.

Revelations about Marianne Foyster and an extraordinary life were disclosed in a BBC 2 programme in October 1994 which attempted to reunite long lost relatives. A fascinating saga of Marianne's several marriages, one bigamous, and adopted and abandoned children, unfolded when her adopted daughter was reunited with her own abandoned son! Marianne's period at Borley was obviously only part of a bizarre life which ended on 18th December 1992 when she died, aged 92.

The Devil Dog of Ingatestone and Others

HE had a menacing, unblinking stare, his eyes brown and shiny as humbugs, and there was something in the set of that powerful jaw that said Here comes danger!

'Fought most of the dogs in the neighbourhood he did. Killed some of them too', volunteered the landlord, 'and some of the cats. A Staffordshire bull terrier he was, no animal ever got the better of him.'

Standing there in the bar of the old Star Inn at Ingatestone, I tentatively stretched out a hand to stroke the smooth head. It didn't require any great show of bravery. I was quite safe, for it is many a long day since the Devil Dog of Ingatestone earned his fearsome reputation. Thanks to the taxidermist's art, his head is mounted above the bar where once he lorded it over lesser creatures.

According to J. Wentworth Day, the writer of many stories about Essex and a Star pub regular, the dog lived at the inn from about 1900 to 1914. 'He would have gone for anything, from a man to a bull. He was one of the last survivors of the old breed of bulldogs,' related Day, and went on to say that although this lion-hearted superdog is now no more, many of the Star's old patrons could vouch for the fact that his spirit lingered on long after his death.

Leslie Smith, who was the landlord when Day was writing for *Essex Countryside* magazine in 1976, had something to say on the subject.

'It happened seventeen years ago when I first took the house over. I came down the lane, opened the side door and my old dog pushed in ahead of me. It's a narrow, dark little passage and leads straight into the bar. The moment my dog set foot in the passage she growled and up went her bristles like a hedgehog. She was dead scared.

'I stood stock still, I couldn't see a thing, but I had the oddest feeling in the world. I knew there was something there, not a yard in front of me, which was challenging the dog – and me. It was trying to stop us entering the house. I knew instinctively it was the spirit of a dog. One could almost see it – black, squatty, teeth bared, blazing with hate, just about to jump and get my dog by the throat or me by the leg ... Then I moved forward. My dog scuttled back behind my legs and the spell was broken.'

Apparently this was not an isolated incident. Other dogs would growl, their hackles up, sensing the hostility of an unseen enemy who apparently still had the power to intimidate although he had been long gone from his former haunts.

The Devil Dog of Ingatestone was once a flesh and blood creature – not so, however, those legendary spectral beasts which roam many a country road or coastal path, big as a calf, their red eyes blazing like bicycle lamps in the gloom. Some say the origin of these fearsome creatures is the hound of Odin, a denizen of the underworld dating back to the Viking invasion, whose many names throughout the country show how widespread is the belief in the existence of the terrifying Black Dog.

In East Anglia he is the Galleytrot, Shuck or Shock, from the old word Scucca, a demon or Satan, and in Norfolk they also call him the Snarleyow. In the North he is Trash, Shriker or the Padfoot and on the Isle of Man they have the Mauthe Doog. In Wales this 'dog of darkness' is called Gwyllgi, and in Yorkshire he is the Barguest.

Most of these canine apparitions are believed to be an omen of death to the person unfortunate enough to encounter them. And on Dartmoor on the B3212 between Two Bridges and Postbridge, an area where there are various supernatural hazards for the traveller to encounter, one of the worst possibilities is to be hunted by the Devil and his pack of hellhounds, snorting fire as they howl hideously in pursuit.

There are Black Dog stories in Suffolk, Norfolk and Cambridgeshire, and, not surprisingly, nearby Essex has had its own encounters with 'Black Shuck'. Between the village and the church in Hockley, north of Rayleigh, there is a stretch of road best avoided on misty nights where a huge spectral hound has frequently been seen padding noiselessly along. The B1026 coast road along by the Blackwater Estuary is another of the Black Dog's haunts, and one summer day in 1960 a cyclist was pedalling northwards along there as daylight was fading. He had passed Tolleshunt D'Arcy when he noticed a large black dog panting alongside. It seemed an unfriendly animal for it snapped and snarled as it ran, and after a while the man swerved his bicycle towards the dog and jumped down, hoping to drive it off.

But as he looked round for his menacing companion, to his amazement he found he was alone. There was absolutely no sign of the dog, which had vanished into thin air, and he was uneasily conscious of a strange, oppressive atmosphere. He stopped for a drink at the nearest pub and mentioned what had happened, but the locals did not seem surprised, and one old man told him he was a fool to ride along that road at dusk in an area with such a long history of super-natural happenings. Apparently he was not the first to encounter the mysterious black hound – and, no doubt, he will not be the last.

This particular area between Peldon and Tolleshunt D'Arcy seems to be a favourite track of the Black Dog, and J. Wentworth Day reported in his *Essex Ghosts* book that a gamekeeper he knew called William Fell had a terrifying encounter when he and a friend were driving in a horse and trap towards Guisnes Court. Near the Salcott cross-roads they suddenly noticed an enormous black dog, its huge red tongue hanging from its mouth. He described it as big as a calf with eyes like bike lamps, and so tall that its head was level with the floorboards of the cart. To their alarm it kept following the cart for about half a mile, then disappeared as suddenly as it had arrived.

A similar encounter happened in the 1920s, to a young girl who lived in Tolleshunt D'Arcy who was sent one frosty, moonlit winter night to fetch the midwife from Tollesbury. She had just cycled past Jordan's Green when a huge black dog, its head level with her handlebars, appeared alongside. She felt cold with fear, the hair rising on the back of her neck as the animal kept pace with her, so close that she could have reached out and touched its rough, shaggy coat. Then when she reached Seabrooks Lane, it disappeared.

On the way back to her relief the road seemed clear, but at Gorwell Hall Lane there it was, lying in the middle of the road. It seemed to be asleep, its bright red tongue hanging out of its mouth, and it was so big it left only a small space where she could pass, but she managed to slip by without disturbing it and cycle home as fast as she could.

Enquiries in the area failed to discover anyone who owned such a dog, and it was many years later that she read about Black Shuck and realised what she had seen.

So what should you do if you meet the Black Dog? Despite the widespread belief that to encounter the super-natural beast is the equivalent of a death warrant, others say that if you show no fear the dog will simply walk along behind you, his huge paws making no sound. But on no account try to run away. There are even brave souls who have attempted to pat the creature, at which point he is said to disappear.

There is another unlikely animal to be seen in Essex that is known as the Shug Monkey. Travellers report its sudden appearance in car headlights on the B1052 Newmarket to Saffron Walden road and if you want to see it, the best place is the stretch between West Wratting and Balsham, just north of the Essex border, in a little-used lane called Slough Hill. People who have seen it describe it as having the body of a large, black, shaggy sheepdog and the face of a monkey with big, shining eyes. Sometimes it has been seen walking erect, and at others it lopes along on all fours at great speed.

Another curious dog story comes from the old White Hart inn at West Mersea where, a few years ago, a cellarman attending to the beer casks almost fell over a dog, which he thought was one of the landlord's pets. He asked the landlord to call it off, but the landlord's two dogs were up in the lounge, and when the cellarman looked round the mystery dog had vanished. The same thing happened later when another cellarman was checking the barrels. He saw a black dog in the cellar and thought a stray must have come in, but the cellar door was still closed as he had left it, and when he looked round the dog had gone although there was no other way out.

There is an old belief that a tunnel runs from the pub cellar to the nearby churchyard, which must have been handy in smuggling days. In times gone by an animal was sometimes sacrificed and buried under the foundations of a building so that its spirit would act as a guardian against evil influences. Is it too far-fetched to wonder if such a dog travels sometimes from the churchyard and through the tunnel to pay the White Hart a visit?

Or was it our old friend Black Shuck? It's only a short distance from his usual beat after all!

The Farm in the Marshes

RELAXING in the comfortable sitting room with a friendly cat on my lap I had no uneasy feelings. And yet I had come to this isolated farm on the Essex marshes to hear first hand about a succession of paranormal happenings here that had at first aroused curiosity in its new occupants but later caused alarm and apprehension. Because everything happened so recently, I have changed the names of those involved in order to preserve their anonymity.

Chris and her husband David moved into the farm with their two year old daughter, Lynn, in the late summer of 1989. 'We've never been tuned into ghosts or been interested in that sort of thing,' Chris told me. 'When we came to live here it was the last thing on our minds, we were so busy getting settled in.' There was a lot to do putting the rather neglected house in order and from time to time when they noticed footsteps outside they assumed it was just someone passing by in the lane. But about three weeks after they arrived, Chris woke in the night to hear the sound of someone walking about right underneath the bedroom window.

'They were very heavy footsteps,' she explained, 'like someone wearing wellingtons, and gave the impression of someone very tall taking long strides.'

David heard them too, and went down to check outside while Chris looked down from the window, but although the heavy tramp of someone walking around close by could still be heard, there was no one to see.

'We found out later talking to neighbours that an old ploughman used to live here, and he was in the habit of walking round the farm at night checking on his livestock,' said Chris. 'And', she went on, 'we think he's still here. Apparently he was a very big man, 6 foot 4 inches tall, and the footsteps we heard certainly sounded like someone tall with a long stride.'

They continued to hear the disembodied footsteps from time to time, but took little notice as now there were the sounds of the farm animals and their four dogs which helped to mask other noises. However, their little girl had started talking to an invisible new friend whom she called John. When asked, she would say he was a nice man, and she chatted away as she sat at her little desk drawing a picture for John. Chris noticed that as she talked, Lynn was looking high up towards the ceiling as if John was up there – or, of course, as if he was very tall!

'We asked her what John looked like', said Chris, 'and she described a man who sounded just like the old ploughman. Neighbours who had known him said what a nice person he was, very much a gentleman. He sounded like someone you would have liked to know, and I feel sure he was not the cause of our problems here.'

As Chris and David started to restock the farm, they let out the stables to various people for their horses, but no one seemed to stay long. 'People said they felt there were often voices calling them by name. They thought it was us, but it wasn't. Some said they were conscious of an uneasy atmosphere they didn't like, and this seemed to be gradually building up.

'I was working in the dairy late one night when I heard my husband call me. I answered, and went out and met him outside as he thought I had called him. We then both distinctly heard a woman's voice call David by name. It seemed to be coming from the pig pens but when we looked round there was no one there, and the animals seemed undisturbed.'

Another strange happening that Chris described is the sound of a car arriving and driving up to the barn. The engine stops and then there is the sound of a car door opening and a woman's voice calls 'COO-ee'.

'It sounds so normal', Chris told me, 'that time and time again I have gone to look but there is no car, and no one there. It is so real that you just accept it is someone arriving.

'I have been told that during the last war women from the WVS used to deliver things to the men on the gun sites here, and once a car drove into the wall outside and crashed. It was a fatal accident and we wondered if this could have something to do with the sounds we hear. It's odd because it sounds as if the car is drawing up on gravel. There isn't any gravel now, and hasn't been for ages, but there was gravel in the yard during the war and early 1950s.'

After about a year, the family started noticing cold feelings throughout the house, and Chris told of an odd sensation of pressure building up that was difficult to describe. Then sometimes when she was working in the kitchen she would notice, out of the corner of her eye, something moving.

'I'd brush back my hair, thinking it was nothing more than that,' she said, 'but it was like a shadow dancing across the hall. Once I was sitting reading and looked up to see a shadow pass along the wall. It was like smoke. And on another occasion I saw a ball shape pass along the bottom of the wall. My husband often complained because I left the lights on all over the house, but a growing feeling of uneasiness was making me jumpy.

'One Christmas I was in the kitchen cooking while my husband went to have a drink with some neighbours. I had the radio on playing carols while I was working, and hadn't noticed how dark it was getting, but suddenly for no reason an awful feeling of depression came over me. I'd never felt anything like it before, I just wanted to curl up and shut everything out. I hadn't been thinking about anything ghostly at all, but now I was becoming really tense and frightened. When my husband came back he switched the lights on and found me hunched up in a corner in the dark.

'After Christmas, I was sitting on the floor by the fire one night and David was outside in the barn. I heard footsteps outside and then the side door opened. I assumed it was David but he didn't come into the room. When he did arrive later I told him what had happened and we thought there might have been an intruder as the sounds had been so real. So we checked the house, but there was no one around.'

As time went on the atmosphere in the house didn't improve. A neighbour who visited them for dinner one night said he thought he saw something like a shadow passing across the hall which made him feel nervous. There was a cold spot in the office which several people noticed. And little Lynn said she saw books and other things move of their own accord, and once she saw a pair of shoes 'walk down the hall'.

'We decided to put the farm up for sale,' said Chris, 'we really didn't want to stay any longer. It seemed an unlucky place, apart from the strange happenings. We were having business problems and we'd lost four healthy young dogs one after the other. But although several people came to look over the farm, we didn't manage to sell it.'

But something had to be done and, feeling that the happenings at the farm were something outside their experience, Chris and David asked their local Roman Catholic minister to visit them.

His first words were 'I sense that you need more than a blessing.' He walked from room to room in the house,

43

saying 'If you come in peace, stay, but if not, be gone', and then said prayers in each room and blessed it. Afterwards he said prayers over each of the family, and blessed them too. He had brought a large crucifix with him and left it with them as a protection and, in fact, they now have a crucifix in every room of the house.

'After he had finished I was amazed at the difference,' said Chris. 'The whole house felt warmer, the atmosphere was lighter, and everyone was happier. It was a pleasure to come home. And when the next fuel bill came it was less than a third of the previous one.'

So is the haunting at an end? Not exactly. Chris told me that if they talk about it to anyone, something always happens. They were out with some friends recently, and an elderly neighbour was babysitting. When they got home she told them that about an hour before there had been a curious scratching noise in the chimney as if a large bird was scrabbling away with its claws. And when they thought about it they realised that it must have been about that time that they were telling their friends about the strange goings on at the farm.

And only a few days before my visit, Chris was discussing the happenings at the farm with someone else and when she arrived home she found that three drinking glasses had been stacked inside each other in the kitchen and the middle one was completely shattered leaving the other two undamaged. What is disturbing the peace of this isolated farm? The old ploughman's footsteps and the sound of the car that never arrives seem simply like echoes of the recent past. But what of the rest?

The farm is set in a lonely area of creeks, rivers and marshland on the edge of the estuary, a part of Essex with a remarkable heritage of strange stories of ancient ghosts, witches and smugglers, not forgetting the spectral black hound of Odin. Even the Prince of Darkness himself apparently figured prominently in the lives of Essex inhabitants centuries ago. Many places still bear his name, like Devil's Wood, Devil's Walls, Devil's Steps and the Devil's Field, and one often told legend is sited close by the haunted farmhouse I visited that day.

It seems that a medieval knight planned to build a house in Devil's Wood but, after a moat had been dug and building started, every night the day's work was demolished. So the knight and his two dogs kept guard one night to catch the culprit, and to his consternation it was the Devil who arrived with his hounds. It's said that the Devil was furious that the knight had chosen to build his house in this wood as it was where he held his revels.

He then picked up a beam and threw it to the top of a nearby hill with the words 'Where this beam doth fall, there build Barn Hall'.

Barn Hall was duly built at Tolleshunt Knights and the 'Devil's Beam' can still be seen in the cellar, with marks on it described as the Devil's clawmarks.

Alas for the knight who had originally chosen such an unfortunate building site; the Devil swore that when he died he would have his soul, whether he was buried inside or outside the church. To thwart the Devil, the knight was eventually interred half in and half out of the wall of the church at Tolleshunt Knights, where some say the scratches on the tomb are due to the Devil's frantic and unsuccessful attempts to reach the knight inside.

Curiously enough, a field nearby known as Moat Field is believed to be the very place where the knight originally intended to build his house. This field has long had a reputation for being haunted, but a young man's experience there around 1980 suggests that local people who give the place a wide berth have good reason.

At the time of this happening the farmer who owned it asked his son to get the field ploughed as soon as they had finished the harvest. It was quite late in the day before the young man was able to start ploughing and he was still at work that evening when dusk had started to fall.

He switched on the tractor's powerful lights and continued his work although the rest of the field was now in darkness. Then suddenly his eye was attracted by a movement out of the corner of his eye, but when he turned his head there seemed to be nothing and he thought he must have glimpsed a passing bird or animal. But almost immediately the flicker of another shadow caught his eye, and then another and another, just momentary sightings as if whatever it was was trying to keep out of view. The young man was becoming alarmed as, turning round, he thought he could see other shadowy forms behind his tractor, and as he twisted this way and that trying to peer through the darkness beyond his tractor's beam, his foot slipped off the pedal, causing the engine to stall, and the tractor lurched to a stop.

Becoming more and more agitated he tried repeatedly to restart his tractor, aware that he seemed to be surrounded by moving shadows. And then, to his horror, he heard a click and saw the door handle begin to move. In a panic he turned the ignition key again, and this time the engine started and he began to drive at full speed across the newly ploughed furrows, bouncing crazily towards the gate, conscious that as the lights illuminated the surrounding field there were shadowy forms just on the edge of his vision. And as he passed the moat and its surrounding woodland the tractor lurched sideways and the lights went out.

Thankful that he had almost reached the gate he suddenly heard the sound of the door handle being rattled. He grabbed it and pushed the lock button as a hefty blow on the side of the tractor shook his cab, then at full throttle he rocketed through the gate and out onto the road and home as fast as he could go.

In the safety of the yard at home he examined the outside of his tractor, and found the right side badly dented and long, deep scratches all round the door handle. After the lad's terrifying experience the farmer sold the field as soon as he could, but that nightmare evening had a lasting effect on his son, who still avoids night ploughing, in fact he is not keen on even driving his car after dark.

So what is the mystery of Moat Field and why do local people say it is haunted? Memories are long in the countryside and folklore often has a basis in fact. In her *Ghosthunter's Guide to Essex* Jessie Payne suggests that the old story of the Devil objecting to the first proposed site of Barn Hall could possibly have had something to do with Devil worshipping rites in pagan times in what is now called Devil's Wood. And those dark menacing shadows in Moat Field that night, what were they?

Essex is a strange county, haunted by the spirits of Romans, Vikings, Crusaders, witches and long dead queens, and more ordinary people like you and me. There are many unexplained mysteries in its lonely places, some almost as isolated as they were centuries ago, and who knows what lurks in the darkness, just out of sight?

Ghosts of Saffron Walden

Town Ghosts

THE Old Sun Inn at Saffron Walden is one of the most attractive buildings in that delightful market town, with its gables and wonderful pargeting, and historic associations with Cromwell at the time of the Civil War. It is no longer an inn but, making the most of its narrow passages and fascinating network of interconnecting rooms, it now houses Lankester Antiques.

The brooding portrait of Oliver Cromwell hangs on one wall, warts and all, but there is no reason to suppose that the shade of the great man still lingers among the innumerable books and antiques which now fill every inch of the ancient building he once knew.

There is, however, a story that the ghost of one of Cromwell's soldiers haunts the old hostelry, and when I spoke to the proprietor he said that sometimes customers say they are conscious of a strange atmosphere in some of the rooms. And others, perhaps more sensitive, find some parts of the building oppressive and cannot bear to stay there. He went on to tell me that one part of the building used to house a small cafe, and one day the couple who ran it arrived looking rather disgruntled. They complained that the noise at night was keeping them awake, and it would be appreciated if the staff could stop moving heavy furniture around so late. The antique dealer assured them that no one had been working in the shop at night but the cafe proprietors said they had knocked on the wall, and someone knocked back, but the noise still went on.

The antique dealer thought he must have had burglars, so went to check the upper rooms, but everything was in order there, so the midnight furniture mover remained a mystery.

Another Saffron Walden hostelry also has Civil War associations. This is the handsome timbered Cross Keys at the corner of King Street and High Street which achieved the distinction of an entry in the American *Good Ghost Guide.*

Theirs is a Christmas ghost who between 11 pm and midnight on Christmas Eve can be heard tramping heavily along a passageway which ends in a blank wall. There is a belief that the invisible entity is one of Cromwell's men who guarded Royalist prisoners held there before being taken on to Colchester, but why he is only on guard duty at Christmas is anyone's guess.

A former Mayor of Saffron Walden, the late Stanley Wilson, wrote in *Essex Countryside* in 1973 about the ghost of Hill House in the High Street. He was able to talk to Violet, one of the last surviving maids, who worked at Hill House many years ago and who knew all about the sad little ghost who 'swished along the corridor and bedrooms, followed by an icy-cold draught, terrifying the younger servants'.

The haunting dated back to 6th January 1845 when Nelly Ketteridge, a 19 year old maid, set off from Hill House to walk to her home at Elmdon on her day off. But on the way she was caught in a heavy snowstorm and her body was found six weeks later in a ditch between Wendens Ambo and Wenden Lofts, a victim of hypothermia.

Mr Wilson's friend Violet said that the older servants took no notice of Nelly's ghost which had haunted Hill House for many years, accepting her as part of the family, but Violet used to leave her bedroom door open at night hoping for a glimpse of the ghost that could be heard but not seen.

The Moat Farm Murder

A CENTURY ago, Clavering village, not far from Saffron Walden, was associated with what newspapers of the time called 'The most sensational criminal trial of modern years'.

Miss Camille Holland, a well-to-do spinster of 56, met Herbert Samuel Dougal, 55, through an advertisement in a matrimonial paper. She was not to know that he was a bigamist and a criminal who had served a prison sentence for forgery, and Camille was soon swept off her feet by this well-built, bearded charmer who posed as an ex-army officer. On 27th April 1899 they moved into Moat Farm, Clavering which he had persuaded her to buy.

But three weeks later Miss Holland mysteriously disappeared as if she had vanished into thin air. On the evening of 19th May 1899 Camille and Dougal had gone out in the pony trap but he returned alone and told Florence Blackwell, the maid, that her mistress had gone to London but would be back soon. During the evening he went out several times, telling Florence he was going to meet Camille from the train, but he returned alone and early next morning Dougal told Florence that he had received a letter from her mistress saying that she had decided to have a little holiday.

Florence, who had complained to Camille about Dougal's attempts to kiss and molest her, had no intention of remaining in the house alone with him and left hurriedly that morning.

It was April 1903 before the truth emerged about Camille Holland's fate. In the meantime Dougal had moved his 'widowed daughter' into the farm, a lady afterwards identified as his wife, and a succession of cheques purporting to be signed by Miss Holland had issued from the farm. Neither the bank or Miss Holland's relatives appear to have had any suspicion that all was not well, but eventually local gossip did cause the police to make discreet enquiries as it was so long since Camille had been seen, and some even thought she might be a prisoner in the house.

Dougal was arrested and charged with forgery, and meantime the maid Florence Blackwell was interviewed. She was able to tell them of the curious happenings on the night her mistress unexpectedly disappeared, leaving behind her clothes and belongings. The moat was excavated and Camille Holland's body found. It transpired that when the couple returned from their drive on 19th May 1899, Dougal stabled the pony and while Camille stood admiring the moonlight he came up behind and shot her, later burying her in the moat.

Dougal was tried at Chelmsford and in less than an hour the jury found him guilty of murder. He was hanged on 14th July 1903.

Not surprisingly, a house where such events have happened is an obvious focus for ghost stories. Not long after the trial a local blacksmith passing by Moat Farm one night was surprised to hear the sound of a piano being played just as Camille Holland used to do. But now the house was empty, and needless to say, he hurried by.

In her book *Favourite Haunts*, Jean Gumbrell relates the experiences of a farmer's family who lived at Moat Farm later, around the time of the First World War.

A room over the kitchen was used to store tools, and one night the family in the kitchen heard a terrible racket as if all the tools were being thrown about. But when they went to investigate nothing had been touched and all was quiet.

On another night the farmer was in one half of a divided barn with a cow that was calving when a tremendous noise started up in the other half. Yet again, when he checked nothing was disturbed.

There were other times when they would hear the front door open and shut repeatedly when no one was there, and sometimes they would be woken in the night by the same sound of the front door opening and closing although they knew it had been locked and bolted.

On the night that Dougal shot Camille, he left her body where it fell and went indoors for a drink of brandy. He told a journalist later that he went out several times intending to bury the body, but couldn't face it and had to go back to the house for another drink. This explains his comings and goings when he told the maid Florence that he had been to the station to meet Camille.

So when the family living at Moat Farm heard the door mysteriously opening and closing when they knew it was locked, perhaps it was Dougal's restless spirit re-enacting the events of the terrible night of the Moat Farm murder?

Mysterious Mersea and Other Islands

THE Rev Sabine Baring-Gould, once the rector of East Mersea, on Mersea Island, used to complain that it was always cold there. And who would argue with him in wintertime when a keen wind comes roaring across the North Sea, howling like a lost soul, and strange lights like will-o'-the-wisps flicker on the misty marshes. It is an eerie and mysterious place then when one can readily believe Mersea's many ghost stories, some dating back to the days when it was a Roman outpost.

Ghosts of those old Romans still linger in the area, as Baring-Gould himself had reason to believe when he heard the steady tramp of a troop of foot soldiers approaching one night and yet there was nothing to see. This was no surprise to local people who had often heard the 'marching footsteps'. But most famous of all is the Roman centurion who has been both heard and seen over the centuries, as he comes marching over the Strood, the causeway that links Mersea to the mainland.

Mrs Jane Pullen, former landlady of the charming old Peldon Rose inn, was escorted by the ghost one night when she was on her way home. 'He came down off the Barrow Hills,' she said. 'The steady tramp of a man's feet, like it was a soldier marching, and he caught up with me and walked all the way down to the Strood. I could see no one, yet the feet were close behind me, as near as I could have touched him.

'I bopped down to look along the road in the moonlight, yet no one was there. Still the feet kept on.'

She met a man she knew who was terrified by their invisible companion, but the stalwart old lady told him "'Tis only one of those old Romans, come out of the Barrows to take his walk.'

And they walked on, with the footsteps beside them, until they turned off towards the Peldon Rose and the sound continued on.

A huge mound of earth at Barrow Farm was excavated many years ago and a lead casket containing a glass bowl with human ashes inside was found, which is now in Colchester Museum. Do they have some connection with the ghostly centurion who marches down to the Strood?

One motorist crossing the Strood narrowly avoided hitting a figure which emerged suddenly from the mist, and two naval ratings had a similar experience in February 1970, but in their case they had driven through it before they could stop. But there was no bump, no damage and no body! Other figures believed to be Roman soldiers have been seen on the East Mersea road, and the Rev Baring-Gould used to say that on certain nights you could hear the sound of clashing swords and battle cries, an echo of the time when the Roman legions fought their way ashore.

Ray Island, part of a group of small islands off Mersea Island, also knew the Romans, as a young man had reason to know one moonlight night when he camped out there. He woke in the middle of the night to hear someone tramping towards him but when he looked out there was no one about, and yet the measured soldierly tread continued right up to his tent – and on – which frightened him so much that he left it and his belongings behind and ran for home.

Canvey Island, too, has its ghosts of long ago as fishermen and wildfowlers of Canvey Point know for some of them speak of the famous Viking who stalks the saltings, a lonely relic of the Danes who invaded the Essex coast more than a thousand years ago. He must be a striking figure to encounter, standing six feet tall, with long moustaches and a beard, wearing a leather jerkin and a winged helmet on his head, his long sword hanging from his belt.

East Mersea has its curiosities as well as ghosts, and in the churchyard the visitor may come across something quite unusual. It is an old metal cage fixed over the ground with a plate bearing the words 'Sarah Wrench Died May 6th 1848 Aged 15 years & 5 months'. The local story is that Sarah Wrench, young as she was, was much feared as a witch in the neighbourhood, but how or why she died so young is not recorded.

Some say, reasonably enough, that the metal cage fixed over her grave was to thwart body snatchers, but why was only one grave protected in this way? Others suggest that it had the more sinister purpose of preventing Sarah's ghost from walking. Was she really a witch? Who can say, except to note that her grave is on the north side of the church, often an unconsecrated area where, in the old days, suicides and wrongdoers were buried. Also, at the time the witch persecution mania was at its height, in the 17th century, it was the custom for executed witches to be buried in uncon-secrated ground with their heads to the north. What did happen to Sarah Wrench?

The Essex coast is still a mysterious area these days, with its special heritage of strange stories of ghosts, witches and smugglers, even the Devil himself. But it has its own, distinct charm for those who love its wildness, its wide skies and lonely marshes, and the sensation that echoes of more ancient times are still there for those who are aware of them ...

Two Cunning Men and Some Witches

IF you had lived in Hadleigh in the first half of the 19th century, and had serious problems, who could you turn to for help? Perhaps your livestock were mysteriously ailing, or a member of your family was 'took comical', with strange hysterical fits, which made everyone shake their heads and mutter 'witchcraft'. Or perhaps your true love had proved faithless.

There was only one answer. Sooner or later you would be knocking on the door of a small clapboarded cottage where the daunting cry 'I am the Devil's Master' told the nervous supplicant that James Murrell the Cunning Man was at home. Inside in a little room festooned with bunches of herbs hung up to dry and littered with books and mysterious charts, there he'd be, a thin, slight figure, no taller than five feet high, wearing his threadbare old blue frock coat with the brass buttons, his sharp blue eyes glittering in the firelight as he keenly eyed his visitor through his iron rimmed spectacles.

In those isolated and superstitious country areas no one questioned the power and authority of Cunning Murrell. He was regarded with respect bordering on fear and in his home village of Hadleigh and in Canewdon, to the north-east, stories about him were remembered for many years after his death in 1860. A book – *Cunning Murrell* – by Arthur Morrison, published in 1900, is described on the title page as a tale of witchcraft and smuggling, but I suspect today we would call it 'faction', as Morrison collected many a curious story of Murrell and his mysterious activities to use in his novel. When Morrison visited Hadleigh just twenty-five years after Murrell's death, he was in time to talk to Murrell's youngest son Edward, known as Buck, as well as the blacksmith who once made Murrell's famous iron witch bottles.

In his youth Murrell had worked for a London chemist, where he acquired a useful knowledge of pharmacy, and he understood the value of different herbs and natural cures. He had an old box where he hoarded his precious books and papers. There were ancient medical volumes, a Culpeper herbal, books on astronomy, astrology, conjuration and geomancy, all well thumbed and grimy. And a curious volume by a 17th-century wizard called Neoboad. This contained arcane knowledge on charms and spells, together with old horoscopes. To this Murrell had added, in tiny handwriting, his own notes, including a horoscope for Queen Victoria.

It was these treasures that I went to Southchurch Hall Museum in Southend hoping to see. There is a medieval carved wooden chest on view which belonged to Murrell, but the hoard of books, papers and letters which Morrison was lucky enough to see was apparently burnt long ago by some member of the Murrell family.

In an article by Arthur Morrison published in the *Strand Magazine* in 1900 he related the stories local people in Hadleigh and Canewdon told him about Murrell's amazing powers. 'He could do anything, cure anything and know anything, past, present and future,' they declared and forty years after his death at the age of eighty his reputation as a white wizard was undiminished. Whether it was a simple matter of lost property or the defeat of some wicked neighbourhood witch, this remarkable seventh son of a seventh son was the man local people could consult with confidence. Some even whispered that he could fly through the air and be in several places at once. And he had a penetrating glass with which he could look through walls, although those who said it was all done with mirrors maybe knew a thing or two!

Not surprisingly, some of his cases were so extraordinary that they have never been forgotten. There was Sarah Mott of High Street, Hadleigh, cursed by witchcraft so that she ran round in circles without stopping and walked upside down on the ceiling like a bluebottle! Among the papers found after Murrell's death were full details of the charms and other methods he used to effect a cure. And a friend of Murrell's who had had a confrontation with a witch and feared retribution was told by the old wizard to follow her over the heath where she lived and stick a knife into her footprints! When the man did this, the witch cried out in pain and 'hopped all the way home'.

The vital item in defeating the machinations of witches and lifting spells was an iron bottle, made for Murrell by the local blacksmith. Into it went blood, nail clippings, and snippets of hair from the victim, pins, horse nails and some of Murrell's special herbs. This mixture was heated up in the fire at the victim's house, in the belief that as the contents of the witch bottle boiled, the witch herself would feel burning until the spell was lifted.

One day the victim was a Hadleigh girl who had fallen foul of an old gipsy whom she found stealing beer. She sent the old woman packing, but almost immediately started screaming like a cat and barking like a dog as she ran round on all fours! As Murrell conducted his witch bottle ceremony someone was heard coming up the path and a voice cried 'Stop, stop, you're killing me'. At that moment the bottle exploded and the victim was cured, but the body of the old gipsy woman was discovered, half burned, lying in the road.

Murrell himself died on the day he prophesied, 16th December 1860. He was buried on the east side of the little

Norman church in Hadleigh with his wife, who pre-deceased him in 1839, and some of his fourteen children, and his memory is still as green as the unmarked grassy mounds in that traffic-bound oasis.

His reputation was so powerful, far beyond the isolated little village where he lived, that local people must have found it hard to believe that Cunning Murrell had gone at last. Indeed for years after his death they say a familiar small figure in an old blue frock coat and hard glazed black hat like sailors used to wear was sometimes seen as the light was fading, gathering herbs from the hedgerows and putting them in a frail basket hanging from the handle of an old gingham umbrella.

Murrell always said 'There will be witches in Leigh-on-Sea for 100 years and three in Hadleigh and nine in Canewdon for ever.'

Canewdon had its own famous cunning man in The Master of Witches, George Pickingill. There is a photograph of him standing outside his cottage door in his shabby old coat, tall black hat in hand, with an expression of such malevolence that one can readily believe that a glance from his icy blue eyes sent shivers down the spine of any villager.

He was said to have such power over the local witches that he had only to stand at his door and whistle, and they all came running! And he inspired such fear in the village that no one ever refused to do his bidding lest he bewitched them. Pickingill's evil eye was believed to have the power to stop machinery and it was said that Old Picky would order his team of familiars or imps to mow a field at great speed while he sat smoking and drinking his beer. Some people avoided passing his cottage by the Anchor inn at night as they said they could see lots of little red eyes staring at them. Were these his imps, or were they just the pet mice he kept?

Like Murrell, Pickingill lived to a ripe old age, dying at 93 in 1909. He went out with a flourish, promising to give them all something to remember at his funeral. Sure enough, when the hearse drew up at the churchyard the two horses drawing it stepped out of the shafts and galloped away!

Canewdon means 'hill of Cana's people' and commemorates Canute's landing there with his Danish army to do battle with Edmund Ironside for the throne of England. The tower of the ancient church of St Nicholas is believed to have been built by Henry V to celebrate Agincourt, a tower tall enough to have been used as a beacon for ships at sea and from which there is a marvellous view of around a hundred square miles of Essex.

But Canewdon's fame is in its connection with witchcraft. Eric Maple, who spent more than a year in the late fifties collecting the witch lore of Canewdon, wrote that 'there is perhaps no other place in the British Isles where the belief in witchcraft survived so long and so late and where legends of the old dark magic were told only a generation ago in the chimney corner. Little wonder that this district has always been known – and still is – as The Witch County.'

It's said that every time a stone falls from the church tower a witch dies, to be replaced by another. The churchyard itself has long been haunted by a ghost believed to be a 17th-century witch who was condemned and executed. She leaves the churchyard by the west gate and goes downhill to the river, sometimes travelling rapidly on a hurdle. She has also been seen by the crossroads and by the village pond. One man described her floating above the road, wearing a crinoline and a poke bonnet, and as she reached him he was violently thrown to the ground. She was seen several times during the last war when this malevolent spook would suddenly appear behind people and knock them down. Some say she has no head, others say that under her poke bonnet she has no face!

One young man riding his motorbike on Larkhill Road in Canewdon encountered a luminous figure standing in the middle of the road. The head was shrouded in mist and he was convinced he had seen the witch ghost from Canewdon churchyard.

And one night the landlord of the Plough and Sail pub in Paglesham was driving home through Canewdon when 'Something black with staring eyes loomed up out of the darkness in front of my car. There is only one way to describe what I saw,' he said, 'it was a witch.'

Hallowe'en has become a night for would-be ghost-hunters to converge on Canewdon churchyard hoping no doubt for a glimpse of the paranormal. The churchyard has other ghosts, a crusader and another female wraith, both reputed to leave their graves to wander the area at times, and there is another local legend that if you run three times round the church at midnight in an anti-clockwise direction you can go back in time! However, of late police have prevented crowds approaching too close to the church at Hallowe'en, much to the relief of local residents. But the village's reputation for supernatural happenings persists. The *Southend Standard* of 30th May 1963 reported that the wife of the then vicar had several times seen the ghost of a young girl standing in the driveway and doors in the vicarage often opened of their own accord.

Is witchcraft still alive and well in Canewdon? There are people who believe that the old black arts are far from dead even today. After all, an ancient tradition says that as long as the tower of St Nicholas church stands there will be witches in Canewdon, and there it still stands just as it has for centuries in the heart of 'The Witch County'.

Ghosts of the Wayside

IT'S true that many well-known ghosts are old-fashioned creatures, apparently endlessly taking part in a shadowy costume drama. Apparitions of Cavaliers and Roundheads are still fighting the Civil War, the restless wives of Henry VIII flit noiselessly between the royal palaces they once knew, and no stately home or manor house worthy of the name lacks its grey or white lady in her shadowy Elizabethan or Victorian garb.

But ghosts do move with the times, not least the phantoms which haunt not only quiet country lanes but busy motorways, and there are many stories of encounters with mysterious hitch-hikers and unexpected passengers whose behaviour suggests to the startled witness that they are not of this world.

Near the Wickford Roundabout on the Southend bypass, a young girl was killed in a motorcycle accident, but by all accounts she is still sometimes seen thumbing a lift. Motorists or motorcyclists who have stopped to help her say that she asks to go to Victoria Circus, Southend, but before they reach her destination they are shocked to find that their passenger has disappeared without trace.

There are several instances of mysterious passengers who simply appear unannounced in the back of a car.

One November afternoon in 1993 a young woman was driving home along the B1052 road between Saffron Walden and Hadstock. Part of the road once formed a section of the runway of the wartime airfield there and as she reached this point she saw a flash of light and heard a siren. Thinking that a fire engine or ambulance would be approaching, she slowed down and looked in her mirror, and to her utter astonishment she could see an American Air Force pilot in flying kit sitting on the back seat. Unable to believe her own eyes, she skidded to a halt and, heart thumping with fright, nervously looked once again in her mirror, but this time the back seat was empty.

She sat there for a few minutes, her thoughts racing, trying to regain her composure. Had she really seen a wartime American pilot looking at her from the back seat of her car? She was familiar with the road and realised that she had stopped the car on a level with the old control tower of the airfield. When she felt calmer, and was reassured that the back seat was as empty as it ought to be, she drove home, trying to convince herself that her imagination had been playing tricks.

But had it? There is a sequel to this strange story. A few days afterwards, while she was cleaning out her car, the young woman picked up a small object from the back seat. It was a button, a button later identified as one from an American flying jacket. If any sceptic feels inclined to dismiss this happening as moonshine, perhaps they should consider the following.

One November afternoon in 1943 Captain Robert Scholz of the 8th USAAF was returning to Little Walden airfield in his Mustang fighter plane. It had developed engine trouble over the Channel, but using all his skill he had managed to reach his base. The emergency services waited anxiously as he circled around, his engine spluttering badly, but at last he approached the runway and landed. The relief of those watching turned to horror as the Mustang suddenly swerved off course and exploded in flames with no chance of saving Captain Scholz's life.

This strange story poses a question not easy to answer.

Could it possibly be that on the fiftieth anniversary of the accident, for one brief moment in time, a young woman passing the site of that tragic event encountered the spirit of Captain Robert Scholz?

Other grim stories are associated with the old Hadstock aerodrome which make it no place to linger on a misty winter's evening. Any motorist approaching Hadstock village on the B1052 is advised to keep going if they notice an airman who appears to be hitching a lift, for if you pause you will discover to your horror that he has no head!

And should you notice a ball of flames rolling towards the old control tower, don't investigate. You are witnessing a ghostly replay of a tragic day in the last war when a young airman was shot down in flames.

Here is another story of someone who found they had unwittingly acquired an unknown passenger. This driver was passing Osyth Priory Gate House, west of Clacton, early one morning in 1991 when, glancing in his mirror, he was amazed to find an unknown middle-aged lady sitting on the back seat. Startled as he was, he registered that she was dressed in clothes of old-fashioned style and wore a hat with a small posy of flowers on one side.

He pulled up intending to ask 'Who are you?', but when he looked round the back seat was empty and his surprise passenger had flown. He got out of the car and looked up and down the road, but no one was in sight, and when he opened the back door of the car and looked inside he immediately noticed a strong smell of violets. He then recalled with a sense of shock the little bunch of flowers on his strange passenger's hat – they were violets of course! But how? Why? And who? Like other drivers who suddenly discover that they are not alone, he was left wondering.

Ghostly passengers are alarming enough, but there are reports of phantom vehicles too. One June evening, at Thorrington, a filling station cashier sat watching her video monitor. There was something she couldn't quite understand. On the screen she could see a car standing on the forecourt with a man beside it, but as she watched it seemed to her that cars coming and going were passing straight through them. She was unable to leave her position, so she asked a customer to look at the monitor and tell her what she saw. The customer said she could see a man and his car on the forecourt, so the cashier asked if she would mind going outside and walking past the car.

The customer went, and on the video monitor the cashier watched her approach the car and apparently walk straight through it! But when she returned, the customer reported to the puzzled cashier that the forecourt was empty! By this time another interested customer had joined them and suggested that there must be something wrong with the monitor or the tape which could be showing a previous recording. So the cashier changed the tape, but when they looked, the car was still there as before. However, this time, after a little while it faded and the cashier thought that was the end of this puzzling happening.

Not so. The same thing happened on the next evening, and the next. The image of the car appeared at around 9 pm as it had done the first time, gradually fading over the course of twenty minutes or so, and eventually it failed to appear at all. There were several witnesses to this odd manifestation but how or why it happened we may never know.

Some of the most alarming encounters on the roads of this country are ghostly jaywalkers who have an unnerving habit of appearing suddenly in front of passing vehicles, causing the driver to slam on the brakes, often too late to avoid a collision. The story is nearly always the same. The shocked driver jumps out expecting to find the pedestrian injured, or worse, but to his amazement there is no body to be found. Was he dreaming? Was it perhaps a shadow or a passing bird which created the illusion? Many an unfortunate driver is left puzzled and shaken by his unnerving experience.

In the mid-1980s a young man was driving from Thorpe-le-Soken towards Clacton. It was a bitterly cold, snowy February night and, travelling down Tan Lane, he turned into Holland Road and almost ran into an eye-catching figure walking along the road.

It was an elderly, thickset man, in a Victorian style overcoat and tall 'chimney pot' hat, and the driver had the impression that he was bearded. He was carrying a walking stick which he held out in front of him as if he were blind.

But when the driver looked back to make sure the old man was all right, there was no one to be seen! There are other reports of sightings of the same figure, and sometimes he is accompanied by a lady who appears to be hooded, but so far no one seems to know who they are.

In 1991 a young lady was driving from Great Holland towards Clacton and as she approached the hump-backed bridge over the railway she and her passenger noticed how misty it was becoming. They were approaching the junction with Tan Lane when she turned to switch off her car radio, and her passenger screamed because in that split second when her attention lapsed a pedestrian had appeared right in front of the car.

She applied the brakes as fast as she could but, as she reported later, 'the man was halfway through the bonnet of the car'. Both driver and passenger felt icy cold as they realised that the man had apparently walked straight through the car! They were convinced they had encountered a ghost, not least because of his unusual appearance. He was wearing a long black cloak and a tall black hat. Remembering the previous story, the area and the man's old-fashioned appearance, was this another encounter with the same ghost?

Yet another Clacton story was reported in the *Sunday Express* in December 1983. Mrs Avins of Jaywick encountered a figure dressed in white shirt and dinner jacket who walked straight into the path of her car and vanished. It was broad daylight and all the four occupants of the car saw him clearly.

'There was no bump and no body after we stopped to look round,' said Mrs Avins.

There are several stories of phantom coaches such as the ghostly coach driven by a headless coachman which drives towards the ruins of Acton Place, near Long Melford. It was once home to the eccentric 18th-century miser, Robert Jennens, who lived like a tramp although he was reputed to be the richest man in England. As the coach reaches the gates to the drive, it vanishes!

A hearse driven by yet another headless driver passes along The Walls at Mistley from time to time and at Audley End, near Saffron Walden, a phantom coach sometimes emerges from the Lion Gate. It sets off along Audley End Road, over the hump-backed bridge and turns right into Chestnut Avenue. Where is it going? Some say it has been seen on the main Newport Road, the B1383.

An old-fashioned cyclist seen on the road near Faulk-bourne Hall, south of Braintree, seems to approach oncoming traffic with lethal intent! After dark he appears suddenly without lights on the wrong side of the road and targets other cyclists, who are sometimes knocked off their bicycles if they cannot avoid him quickly enough.

One night he apparently went too far, and rode towards a motorcyclist. The rider had no chance of avoiding him and went straight through what he soon realised was the notorious phantom cyclist. Shaken by his experience, the motorcyclist rode off as fast as he could go, but no doubt the phantom biker survived to continue his ghostly road rage attacks regardless! So cyclists beware!

Ghostly monks are very prevalent in Britain, and at Christmas 1977 Richard Sage was driving with three friends along St Mary's Lane, near Cranham, now just inside the Greater London boundary, when a figure appeared out of nowhere, crossed in front of the car and disappeared.

Richard's friend Dee Goss, sitting beside him, saw the figure, and both agreed that it wore a hood or cowl and looked like a monk.

Dee said, 'It seemed to have no legs and just floated across the road in front of us. I saw it very distinctly.'

The two friends sitting in the back of the car had not noticed the figure at all.

Then in December 1979 when Richard was driving along at about the same place as before, the figure appeared again and behaved just as it had on the previous occasion. Although the police suggested that he had just seen a local tramp, Richard and his friend disagreed, and it was later found that there had been other sightings at Christmas 1976 and 1978.

Another phantom monk made a number of appearances in 1964 in the vicinity of Holy Cross church at Basildon New Town. Early one January morning two young women were cycling to work at a newly opened Ford assembly plant. As they passed the church a monk-like figure floated across the road in front of them and, terrified, the girls pedalled as fast as they could away from it.

The same thing happened again a few mornings later, but this time the figure stood stock still in front of one of the bicycles and before she could stop herself the rider went straight through it! Afterwards she said, 'The air was cold and clammy. I went numb all over and could not speak.'

Not long after this encounter, a number of women cleaners from the same factory were walking or cycling home in the early hours and they all saw the monk, which one described as 'just floating in deadly silence'.

The monk was a striking figure wearing a crimson gown, and the witnesses agreed that he seemed to emerge from the bushes at the side of the road to pass in eerie silence over the road into the churchyard of 13th-century Holy Cross, where he disappeared among the gravestones.

The story of the monk's early morning appearances was

widely reported in the press, and local residents confirmed that the churchyard of Holy Cross church was believed to be haunted. However, the then curate at the church said he had never seen anything unusual, although he did admit that while in the church at night sometimes he thought he heard sounds in the porch rather like footsteps, but was sure there was a reasonable explanation.

However, he suggested that the witnesses' description of the monk-like apparition could fit a former Basildon rector who later became Dean of a London church, which would account for his crimson gown. Just why this reverend gentleman should have spent the early mornings frightening passing workers is a mystery but when the publicity brought a flock of eager ghosthunters and sightseers to the church-yard it was too much for him, and afterwards the Ford workers were able to travel to work in peace.

The Ghost Now Standing on Platform Two

MALDON station is a striking and unusual building from which trains once departed for Chelmsford, but the line has long since been closed down and the track was demolished in 1964. But apparently no one thought to tell the ghost, who has been seen many times, still waiting on Platform Two for a train that never comes.

Just when she first appeared is not clear, but according to Mr Torrey Andrews, who was the station master at Maldon for two years, she was seen several times as far back as 1958. His wife Muriel told the *People* newspaper in 1975, 'I saw the lady, a white-shrouded figure, four times. She glided up the path towards the waiting room. There were also strange noises at night. My husband slept with a shotgun at the bedside just in case.'

The couple said that the ghost was accompanied by a weird groaning sound and, whenever she was seen, the atmosphere became icy cold.

Their son Brian visited the station after it had been converted into a pub called the Great Eastern, and said that he had suddenly experienced a very cold feeling. 'When I looked at the door leading to the toilets I saw a misty figure,' he remembered. 'I knew it was the ghost.'

Apparently sightings of the mysterious white lady continued to such effect that one barman who experienced the unnatural coldness and sepulchral groaning found it all too much and left in a hurry.

A young barmaid, Christine Stebbings, said, 'I've never seen the lady, but I accept that she exists. I talk to her in my mind, and ask her not to cause trouble.'

Barry Anderson, co-owner of the pub and restaurant at that time (1975), said, 'The place has an inexplicable atmosphere about it, and there's definitely something going on.'

So what is the story behind the long running haunting of Maldon station? No one seems to know why the mysterious white lady lingered around Platform Two. But a builder who helped to convert the station into the pub added a rather macabre footnote. 'When we were pulling up the floorboards where the bar now stands we found a mummy-shaped area of damp soil,' he said. 'Each time we tried to shift it, it resumed its spooky shape and the soil seemed damp to the touch.'

When I visited Maldon recently I found the old station building boarded up and fenced off, and the area up for sale. So have we heard the last of the white lady? Or is she still wandering around the deserted station building uttering her mournful cry? It will be interesting to know if the next purchaser of Maldon station finds that they have acquired a ghost into the bargain.

Another haunted station story comes from Kelvedon. A British Rail Relief Clerical Officer, now retired, used to work at the old Victorian station there and recalls that he arrived to start work at 4.45 am. Shortly afterwards, at 4.55 am, he would hear footsteps walking across the wooden floor of the booking hall, but when he looked outside there was never anyone there.

He noticed that this always happened at the same time, and was puzzled to account for it until one day he was talking to a man who had been a fireman on the old Crab and Winkle line to Tollesbury. This man explained that men going on duty for both the branch line and for the coal trains in the yard had always arrived at 4.55 am – but that didn't explain why the disembodied footsteps could still be heard.

However, the new station has now replaced the old Victorian one and the phantom footsteps disappeared with it.

More unexplained footsteps were heard by a couple in the 1980s when they waited one evening at Ingatestone station for the London train. There was no one else about, and the station seemed uncommonly quiet, when suddenly they heard the sound of someone approaching across the footbridge.

Oddly enough, they were unable to see the owner of the rather heavy footsteps which continued down the stairs and right past where they were sitting and on towards the end of the platform. To hear what appeared to be the invisible man walk by was a distinctly uncanny experience and when their train arrived they couldn't wait to jump in and get away.

The couple never forgot the mysterious footsteps which passed by them that night, and have never found anyone else who has had the same experience. Or did it happen to you too?

The Little Folk in Essex

D O you believe in fairies? Perhaps you too remember sitting on the edge of your seat in the theatre as Peter Pan urged we children to answer 'Yes', and save Tinker-bell's life.

But ask the same question today and you might get a very quizzical look. Though not necessarily in some parts of Essex which are still so remote and strange that tales of unexpected encounters with spectral coaches, vanishing jaywalkers, malevolent witches and red-eyed Black Shuck do not seem so unlikely. In such places there are even reports of sightings of the little folk. These are not always the delightful winged creatures seen in old-fashioned children's books. They are more likely to be small dwarf-like figures of a mischievous and capricious nature. But members of the fairy kingdom they undoubtedly are.

Country people have always had a healthy respect for the little people, and with good reason. Fairies have traditionally been notorious for exchanging their own babies for human children, and mothers fearful of finding a changeling in the cradle would tie a sprig of rowan to the cot, or leave an open bible alongside, or even put a knife or a pair of tongs on the cradle if the baby had to be left alone. There are also tales of people lured away by the fairies to feast and dance the night away, but on returning home next day, as they thought, they found to their amazement that years had passed.

Although our polluted and traffic congested cities may be no place for fairies, stories still surface from the countryside of Ireland, Wales and the West Country which suggest that the little people are still around for those with eyes to see them. I know of an ancient farm in Cornwall where Cornish Piskies 'remarkably like the little brass models you buy in souvenir shops' are still to be seen, and when a new area of woodland was being established there a myriad of tiny glittering fairies appeared flying around the new young saplings in a shining cloud, touching the roots and branches as they were being planted, to help them grow.

And in 1979, the *Daily Mail* reported an encounter between a group of Nottingham children and some gnomes in Wollaton Park! The children had been playing in the park and were on their way home at dusk when they heard 'a tinkly bell' and around thirty little bubble cars driven by gnomes came out of the bushes. 'They were about half my size and looked old,' said one 10 year old girl. 'They had greenish faces with crinkles in them and long white beards. They were laughing in a funny way and driving over swamps near the lake.' The children were frightened and hurried away, but next morning they told their headmaster at school all about it, and he was convinced that they were speaking the truth. A representative of the Fairy Investigation Society of Nottingham also accepted that the children's experience was genuine as she had received other reports of gnome sightings in the park.

A narrow, winding lane between green fields leads to the scattered hamlet of Broxted in Essex. There are some picturesque thatched cottages, a 13th-century church and a windmill, but nothing to suggest that this is one of those rare places in this day and age where the little people have often been seen. Here local inhabitants have described how tiny gnome-like creatures have appeared at dusk and sometimes in broad daylight too. At these times particularly sensitive people have been conscious of a strange sensation in the air like the quivering of invisible wings.

Mr S. John Saunders, who has written about this area in several East Anglian magazines, says that at one Broxted farm tractors have repeatedly broken down for no apparent reason, crops have withered and sometimes tools and equipment have mysteriously disappeared only to reappear a few days later, all mishaps attributed to unfriendly fairy influence. And one day while cycling there, Mr Saunders was almost pitched off into a ditch by an invisible force. For a radio programme he talked to a tractor driver, Keith Foster, who, with his sister Janice, had come upon a 'grimacing dwarf' when they walked into an empty farmhouse. And which was the Broxted cottage, I wondered, where two local women had often witnessed fairies dancing on their kitchen table?

Another local man, Bob Wallace, swore that the little people frequently watched him while he was at work on his small-holding, laughing and teasing him until he threatened to throw clods of earth at them. And yet another man disturbed fairy folk one night in his garden and, apparently annoyed at being seen, they stripped his apple tree bare overnight.

All kinds of mishaps in the Broxted and Tilty area have been laid at the door of the little folk but local people have maintained an indulgent attitude to their mischief and find their presence more of a privilege than a problem.

In Colchester in the 1960s, in Victoria Road, a local inhabitant noticed fairies playing round a fallen tree trunk in his garden and even managed to take a photograph to prove what he had seen.

And in 1976 a Lawford lady had a delightful experience. As she walked down her garden path she was confronted by a tiny figure about a foot high. It was a quaintly dressed little old lady wearing a shawl and bonnet, and tiny button boots. She was holding a small posy of flowers in her hands, and both ladies stood for a little while, eyeing each other in surprise, then with a smile the fairylike figure rose into the air like a miniature Mary Poppins and slowly floated away, pausing en route to wave goodbye!

Yet another sighting of creatures from the fairy world happened in 1982 when two little girls went into the playing field near Jaywick's Frobisher primary school, not far from Clacton. They were walking along to play in their 'camp' in an overgrown ditch at the end of the field when they suddenly noticed two strange dwarf-like figures ahead. These resembled little old men with long white beards and pointy hats, about three feet tall, and they appeared to be busily digging a hole with old-fashioned spades.

They had obviously not seen the two girls, who stood watching, and quite scared by the strange spectacle the girls slowly retreated and continued to watch from further off. At some point the two gnome-like figures disappeared although the girls did not actually see them go, and although they waited for a time, the little men did not come back.

Then the girls cautiously crept back to where they had seen the little men digging, and despite a search there was no sign of any hole, but both were absolutely certain of what they had seen.

Springfield Place near Chelmsford has a long tradition of being haunted by a 'hideous little dwarf' and in January 1946 the *Essex Weekly News* reported its reappearance. At the time the building had been requisitioned by the Ministry of Supply as a hostel for girls employed by the Hoffman Manufacturing Company. Apparently two girls sleeping on the top floor awoke in fright one night complaining that something uncanny had touched their faces. It was discovered that this part of the building had a reputation for being haunted and after the girls' experience the room they had used was kept locked.

As a result of this report in the newspaper, a letter was published afterwards from a Mary Petre whose grandparents had lived in Springfield Place for many years. She quoted from a book written by Lucy Petre, a relative, who describes what an uncanny place it was then with trap doors, mysterious cupboards high up on the wall that were never opened, dark passages and a secret underground chamber, probably a priest's hole.

There was a large bedroom known as the Blue or Ghost Room. One night Lucy's mother was looking after her baby, Nellie, who was restless due to teething, and they went to sleep in the Blue Room so as not to disturb Nellie's father. The mother was woken later hearing the baby chuckle and call out 'funny man, funny man!' She was alarmed to see a hideous little man standing with folded arms and his back to the fire, and instinctively pulled the bedclothes over her head. She soon threw them back, however, and got out of bed, but the goblin-like figure had vanished, although the baby was still repeating 'funny man' and seemed very amused.

Was it a ghost or some kind of goblin? In his book *Haunted Britain*, A. Hippisley Coxe suggests that it could have been an elemental, but in view of other sightings of similar little characters in Essex, the Springfield Place 'funny man' could possibly have been someone from the fairy world.

A similar creature surprised the new owner of an old house beside woodland on the fringe of Capel St Mary, just over the border in Suffolk. The house had been in a run-down and semi-derelict condition when a London barrister bought it, and he had enjoyed renovating it and bringing it back to habitable condition.

One weekend he travelled there ahead of his family, hoping to finish a few things before his wife and children arrived next day. He was quite late going to bed, but was soon woken up to hear his name being called. He got up and went downstairs thinking that perhaps his family had arrived early after all, but there was no one waiting outside, so feeling puzzled he went back upstairs.

There was an open trapdoor in the ceiling of his bedroom where he had been doing some work earlier, and as he glanced up he was stunned to see a tiny man sitting on the edge of the opening, happily swinging his little legs to and fro. He was about two ft tall, dressed in a green shirt, brown leather breeches with braces, long stockings and boots, with a small trilby type hat on his head. The barrister stared incredulously, and for a brief period the little man stared back, then suddenly vanished!

The barrister was not the type of man to make up such a story. Unlikely as it seemed, he swore that he really had seen what appeared to be a fairybook brownie or goblin. And the matter didn't rest there. When he made a few discreet enquiries in the area, he found that previous occupants of the house had reported sightings of fairies and 'hobgoblins', both indoors and out, but as neighbours thought them rather an odd lot, no one had believed their stories!

So many quiet and lovely places have been eaten up by vast motorways, housing developments, supermarkets and shopping malls, and yet from time to time some unwary citizen finds themself face to face with someone straight out of a children's fairy tale. Are they dreaming? Perhaps fairies and goblins and the rest have been there all the time, but it is only certain people at certain times who can catch a glimpse of them.

Perhaps, to be on the safe side, next time Peter Pan asks 'Do you believe in fairies?' we should join in with the children, and shout 'Yes'!

A Knight to Remember

D ANBURY church can be seen for miles, standing as it
does on one of the highest hills in Essex. Our pagan
ancestors would have chosen a place like this for their
sacred ceremonial bonfires, such as the celebration of St
John's Eve at midsummer, and when the church was built
there in Christian times it was dedicated to St John the
Baptist.

The church has a dramatic history and ancient records
tell of two visitations by the Devil. On Corpus Christi day
in 1402 during evensong there was a violent storm which
broke part of the steeple and damaged the chancel. At the
height of the tempest the Devil himself was seen 'in the
likeness of a greie frier, behaving himselfe verie outra-
geouslie' which naturally put the congregation in 'a marvellous great fright'.

During another legendary visit the Devil stole the fifth
bell from the belfry. This was the bell tolled to mark the
passing of a soul and to drive away the powers of darkness,
and as his satanic majesty fled with his trophy, the close
pursuit of the local people caused him to drop it so that it
rolled down to a place still known as Bell Hill Wood.

It is said that when the fifth bell was replaced no
bellringer could be persuaded to ring it in case this inspired
the Devil to make yet another unwelcome visit to Danbury
church. But Devil or no, Danbury's wooden steeple was the
victim of another violent storm in 1749 when it was struck

by lightning, which burnt the top twenty feet, and during the last war the church was bombed by an enemy aircraft in 1941 causing extensive damage and removing the roof.

Fortunately Danbury's three carved wooden knights were left unharmed, although when I visited the church recently I saw that one seems to be suffering from woodworm and has lost part of one leg.

Who are they, these oaken gentlemen, sleeping the centuries away? A notice in the church states that their armour dates the two in the north aisle as around 1272–1307, the one in the south aisle a little later. Their crossed legs indicate Crusaders or church builders, and as the last Crusade was in 1270 they are assumed to be members of the St Clere family who first endowed the church and were responsible for rebuilding the north aisle.

But Danbury church holds another intriguing mystery, revealed in 1779 when some workmen digging a grave in the north aisle made an interesting discovery. About three feet down they came upon a stone slab and beneath that was a lead coffin. The rector, the churchwarden and the village doctor were summoned and in a state of great excitement the three arrived, under the impression that as the coffin was buried beside one of the church's ancient wooden effigies, inside would be found the remains of a knight of the St Clere family. Impatient as they were to investigate, the three gentlemen contained themselves while they waited for Dr Gower, a famous Chelmsford antiquary, to join them, but when he didn't arrive three days after the discovery of the coffin they decided to go ahead without him.

In 1789, Mr White, the doctor, wrote a full report for the *Gentleman's Magazine* so that we have a blow by blow account of what happened next. The lid of the lead coffin was prised off with a crow-bar, to reveal another coffin of elm wood, in perfect condition. Inside this they found a cement shell three-quarters of an inch thick, and when this in turn was opened, they gazed in astonishment at the incorrupt body of a young man apparently claimed by death in the prime of life. His skin was white and firm, although the face and neck were slightly discoloured and part of one arm was decayed, he had a set of perfect white teeth in his pink gums and the body appeared to show no sign of disease or injury.

In his linen shirt with ruffles at the neck he lay partly immersed in a honey coloured liquid, floating with strange herbs and flowers and a few feathers from the pillow beneath his head which had disintegrated.

The body measured five feet long and was hard to the touch, and the three witnesses decided that it had been embalmed before being immersed in the liquid which partially filled the coffin. This liquid had a slight, delicate smell, and as Mr White possessed no sense of smell, nothing daunted he decided to taste it, describing it as 'aromatic, though not very pungent, partaking of the taste of mushroom catchup and of the pickle of Spanish olives'.

Not content with this, the three men each ripped off a strip of the corpse's shirt as a memento, and then allowed the curious parishioners into the church to view the body. By now, Dr Gower, the antiquary, had joined them and they all agreed that this must be the body of the knight whose wooden effigy lay close by.

Since that appeared to be the end of the matter, the trio of cement, wood and lead coffins were closed down and sealed, and returned to the former position in the north aisle.

But when Mr White's account appeared in print, antiquary Joseph Strutt, the local MP for Maldon, was not convinced about the pickled knight's identity. It was his opinion that this method of preserving bodies was not in use in England until the 15th century and the armour of the wooden figure dated it as late 13th or early 14th century. To prove his point, he opened the tomb beneath the wooden effigy and found, as he expected, a skeleton which had been interred in 13th-century fashion without a coffin or shroud. Since there seemed no doubt about the identity of these remains, Mr Strutt's detective instincts now turned to the true identity of the mysterious body in the mushroom catchup!

He dug down to the pickled knight's grave and found that the outer lead coffin had no inscription of any kind but the stone slab which covered it had a cross fleury and appeared to have once had a brass plaque. Mr Strutt thought this must probably have been the one mentioned by the historian Weever, which had read 'Hic Jacet Geraldus quondam filius et heres Geraldi Braybroke Militis qui obiit xxix Marci MCCCCXXII', Here lies Gerald, once the son and heir of Sir Gerald Braybroke who died 29 March 1422.

Mr Strutt would have been interested to know that when St Paul's was being restored after it had been damaged in the Great Fire of London in 1666, the coffin of Gerald's uncle, Robert, Bishop of London, was opened and the body found in perfect condition, preserved in the same fashion as the body in Danbury church. Robert had been buried in 1404, eighteen years before the death of his nephew, so that this method of preserving a body would have been known to the family.

In his absorbing book *The Knights of Danbury*, Andrew Collins has researched the history of the St Clere family and disagreed that the embalmed knight was Gerald de Braybroke. In his opinion the most likely candidate was William St Clere, Lord of the Manor of Danbury and one of the wooden effigies in the north aisle of the church. He was Sheriff of Essex and Hertford in 1279 and died in 1283.

We do not seem to know the age of William, but the body seen in 1779 was described by an eye witness as 'a hearty youth' so was he perhaps rather young to have been the Sheriff four years earlier? And what of the bones Mr

Strutt found in the logical place, beneath the 13th or early 14th-century wooden effigy in the north aisle?

It seems as if the mystery of the pickled knight of Danbury has still some way to run.

Turpin Rides Again

GEORGE BORROW, writing in the 19th century, called Epping the 'loveliest forest in the world' and although in size it is now only a tenth of its former glory it is still green and beautiful, whether you go there to explore its woodland glades and ancient tracks or, like me, to follow the trail of a notorious desperado, who with his gang of fellow ruffians once infested the forest. In the 18th century the forest was no place to linger admiring the scenery. Outlaws, deer stealers and highwaymen lay in wait for the unwary, and mention of the Waltham Blacks, as the Epping gang were called, was enough to strike terror into the heart of any traveller obliged to pass through the forest after nightfall.

Thanks to books and films the highwayman has acquired a romantic image. He is seen as a dashing figure, daring and courageous, the most famous of them all being Dick Turpin, a local Essex lad born in 1704 at the Bell inn in Hempstead, east of Saffron Walden, where his father was the landlord. It is a little disappointing to find him described as no more than 5 foot 9 inches tall, with a scowling, pockmarked face, and there is little doubt that his tough, brutal nature matched his appearance.

When he was old enough he was apprenticed to a Whitechapel butcher, but it is said that the brutality of his manners got him the sack. He then worked for a time for a Plaistow farmer, but stealing cattle and butchering them for sale brought him to the attention of the law and, after escaping their clutches, he threw in his lot with a gang of smugglers working between Plaistow and Southend.

His next career move was to join forces with highwayman Tom King. They became the terror of Epping Forest to such effect that there was soon a price of £200 on Turpin's head. He had found time to marry an East Ham girl, Hester Palmer, and lived with her in a cottage at Sewardstone, south of Waltham Abbey, but it soon became too risky to be seen there and it was then he made use of a cave at nearby High Beach, well hidden from the road, making secret trips home for food when the coast was clear.

This cave was below the level of the road, disguised by brambles and bracken, and an old print shows Turpin at the cave mouth confronted by a forest keeper unfortunate enough to discover his hideout, as without hesitation the highwayman shot him dead. Years after Turpin's time a small alehouse called Turpin's Cave was built beside it, and in the bar they displayed an interesting collection of objects discovered when the floor of the cave was excavated. There were old horseshoes, a cutlass, a flintlock pistol, padlocks, rusty handcuffs and a pickaxe, relics believed to have belonged to the legendary villain.

Surprisingly, after around 250 years, the cave still looks the same. Some years ago the old inn was demolished and a modern house built on the site. Recently, I visited the owner, Mrs Dawn Moor, who has lived there for some time with her family. Knowing that the shade of Turpin is reputed to haunt a number of his old stamping grounds, I wondered if he still paid an occasional ghostly visit to his former hideaway.

Dawn told me that soon after they moved in she experienced what she described as seeing visions in her mind's eye of a face in the cave. Then one day a man came to see the cave and asked her, 'Where is the carved face of Dick Turpin? It should be in the cave.' Sure enough, to her surprise they were able to discern what is said to be a self portrait by Turpin himself cut into part of the arched entrance to the cave.

Dawn showed it to me, and although you might not notice it at first as you glance inside the cave, once it has been pointed out, the carving is clearly recognisable as a face with well-marked eyebrows, eyes, a broad, flat nose and thick lips. It is a coarse, cruel face one would certainly not like to encounter in real life. It reminded me of the reaction of an eye witness who, after seeing the ghost of Turpin ride through the wall of a house at Aspley Guise in Bedfordshire, one of his well-known refuges, commented that the highwayman looked a much tougher character than he had expected.

Dawn said, 'Once I had seen this carved face in the cave, I never had the visions again.'

There have certainly been hints that the shade of the famous highwayman may still linger in the area of Essex he knew so well. One night Dawn's daughter was driving home and as she was nearing High Beach she noticed a white, misty shape on the road ahead of her. As she drew nearer she could see it resembled a figure on horseback, but it was quite transparent and disappeared as she reached it.

Dawn and her husband have also seen a white, shadowy figure by the front garden fence near the entrance to the cave. 'We both saw it,' she said, 'then as soon as we noticed it, it was gone.'

The family have observed that one room in the house sometimes feels unnaturally cold, and they have all experienced an odd sensation, of 'something not quite right' there. Dawn's younger daughter said that when she and her sister were small they were very much aware of these feelings, and she sometimes had the impression that there were several unseen people in the room.

Turpin ranged far and wide during his notorious career, and there are stories in many places suggesting that at certain times the ghost of the famous highwayman returns to ride again in his old haunts. The *Essex County Book* relates that Turpin on Black Bess is supposed to have leapt the moat at a remote farm at Wimbish, called Tiptofts.

One of his most cruel exploits is remembered at Trap's Hill, Loughton, where his ghost is reputed to return three times a year. Turpin had reason to believe that the old lady who lived at Trap's Hill Farm kept money in the house, and one night he broke in and terrorised her, demanding to know where it was hidden. When she resisted he tortured her by holding her over the kitchen fire until she was forced to give in and Turpin stole £400 and her jewellery. His ghost is said to ride down Trap's Hill hell for leather, and at some point the wraith of an old lady leaps up and clings on behind him, shrieking mournfully. Another version of the story says that after stealing the old woman's money and jewellery, he rode off, dragging her behind his horse until she was battered to death.

Turpin had many ways of foiling the law, and he used a stable at Buckhurst Hill, behind a house called Luctons. There was a closet on the first floor of the house which opened out of one of the bedrooms which Turpin used as another stable, and whenever he arrived there just ahead of his pursuers, he would lead his horse upstairs and hide it in the closet, then bring another horse downstairs to the outside stable. When his pursuers arrived they would find what was obviously a fresh, unridden horse in the stable, and Turpin lounging about nearby, an insolent smile on his face.

He is believed to have had another 'safe house' in Ilford which later became the Green Man inn and, later still, a private residence. A lady who lived in this house as a child says that when her family moved in they found an upstairs room with rings on the walls where horses had been stabled and the stables outside were haunted. From time to time they would hear the sound of a horse galloping up to the gates, but when they went outside to open them, there would be no one there.

Haunted Rochford

WHEN it comes to the ghost with the most – haunts that is – Anne Boleyn seems to be one of the most active with a widespread schedule of appearances around the country. There have been several dramatic sightings at the Tower of London since she was beheaded there in 1536, and she has been seen at Hever Castle in Kent, Bollin Hall in Cheshire and Blickling Hall in Norfolk, where the hapless Queen arrives annually on the date of her death in a coach drawn by headless horses, sitting inside with her head on her lap. It is said that the inhabitants at Blickling are so used to her regular appearances that they no longer take any notice. Poor Anne!

In Essex she has returned in spirit to New Hall at Boreham, perhaps remembering happier times there when Henry still loved her, and also to Rochford Hall, her old family home, where Henry came to court the dark haired beauty he called 'My Lady Anne of Rochford'. According to A. Hippisley Coxe's *Haunted Britain*, Anne's headless ghost haunts Rochford Hall, particularly on the twelve nights following Christmas.

There is much mystery surrounding Anne Boleyn, such as where she was born and also her final resting place. After her execution history relates that her body was unceremoniously dumped in an old arrow chest and buried in the chapel of St Peter ad Vincula in the Tower of London. And since a ghostly procession has sometimes been seen in the chapel led by a figure closely resembling Anne Boleyn, this would seem to add credence to this belief.

But a tradition persists that Anne's heart (or some say her

head) was removed from this grave and, after a brief pause at Rochford Hall, was reburied at East Horndon church which stands on a hilltop adjacent to the Southend arterial road, the A127.

Whether or not she did haunt Rochford Hall, an obstreperous ghost of some kind was causing trouble there in the 18th century, reported by the Rector of Woodham Mortimer in a letter in August 1776: 'The Rochford Hall Ghost grows more rude every day. He now amuses himself with throwing the boots and shoes at the men's heads. Mr. Wright was at Rochford the week before last and sent in a great hurry for Mr. Codd and me to come to exorcise this riotous Ghost but I was unluckily in Town.'

The town of Rochford has another ancient building, where restoration work in 1983 apparently activated a whole collection of apparitions. This is the 13th-century property in South Street known as The Old House and now used as council offices, and after builders working on it described ghostly sightings a group headed by Jacqueline English, then a trainee with Rochford District Council, decided to spend the night there in September 1984. 'I talked to a former resident who told me she and her family had seen several strange figures, as well as hearing loud wheezing in one of the bedrooms,' she told the local press.

Miss English has written a booklet about the historic gabled building which had originally been assumed to date from the 15th century, but during the extensive restoration work evidence was revealed that its real age was approximately 1270. Obviously through the centuries the house has known many occupants and happenings and it would not be surprising if echoes of the past still lingered there.

And so on a warm September evening Jacqueline English and five other people including Carol, a psychic, arrived at The Old House armed with sleeping bags and flasks of coffee, hoping that any paranormal phenomena there would make themselves known.

After holding a meditation in the main hall, the group exchanged impressions they had picked up. Several people had been conscious of presences, one a woman in a black and white dress of Puritan appearance with children and a dog, and several other vague figures. Later some members of the group described scenes seen in the mind's eye that seemed like glimpses of the past, such as someone lying in bed with an old lady in bonnet and shawl also there, apparently knitting. There was also a table laid for a banquet, and a happy group of Quakers singing.

Carol, the psychic, had more dramatic visions to report. She described a screaming woman and men committing a murder, a frightened woman under arrest begging for a pardon and, most vivid of all, a delightful little Victorian girl in a long dress, holding a rag doll. She felt that the child probably died young in the house.

During a solitary tour of the house Carol received more impressions, as if the previous life of the house had impregnated the fabric of the building and had been somehow activated by the recent building and restoration work. After a midnight meditation in the main hall, she noticed the same little girl coming down the stairs and walking towards her. The child had blonde hair in ringlets and told Carol she was looking for her mother. Carol sensed that the child's name was Lizzie and she was six or seven years old, and when asked how she died, the answer was 'a bad cough'. Lizzie seemed to be afraid of a hovering presence she called 'the man in green' and, believing that poor little earthbound Lizzie wanted release, Carol told her to 'walk towards the white light'. She then saw her disappear through the dormer window and said she had gone towards the light and to waiting arms.

Carol then concentrated on the man in green who had been nearby as she was talking to Lizzie. She described his green velvet suit, pouch and hat as medieval and said he seemed angry and was shouting 'Get out of my house'.

When asked who he was, he replied, 'I am the Lord of all that you see.' She was also aware of a figure in black Elizabethan garb drawing a long thin sword, and another member of the group saw the Puritan lady again, but more clearly this time.

It was a long and interesting vigil in which some of the group, particularly the sensitive Carol, seemed to have tuned in to a kaleidoscope of the house's past.

Some time before the September visit Jacqueline had talked to previous occupants who described their sightings of a little girl of six or seven in a long white nightdress who wandered around the house, often weeping, and it seemed likely that she was one and the same as the child ghost Lizzie who appeared during the vigil. These people had heard heavy breathing in a bedroom that since renovation is now part of the main hall, and the dormer window through which Lizzie disappeared was once in that room. Were the wheezing noises reported due to poor Lizzie's last illness?

When I talked to Jacqueline English (now McEwan) recently, she mentioned the man in green. 'He seemed as if he wanted to make contact,' she said. 'He appeared in various parts of the house during the vigil.'

Since the house has been converted to council offices it is open to visitors on Wednesday afternoons from 14.00 to 16.30, with guided tours available. Jacqueline acted as a guide while working at The Old House but experienced nothing paranormal then and the staff who work there at present have never seen any ghostly apparitions.

Restoration and building work frequently stir up paranormal activity in old property. It is as if scenes, often of violence or passion, leave such a strong impression on their surroundings that in certain circumstances they can be replayed like a recording. Any figures present appear oblivious of anyone watching, whereas what I think of as 'real ghosts', such as Lizzie or the man in green, react to a living human presence and even communicate.

How does it work? If only we knew, and could re-activate what someone has called the cinema of time at will and see the past unroll like a magic picture show. Meantime The Old House at Rochford is a wonderful building, full of history – and secrets.

The Beautiful Bigamist

THE story of Catherine Canham is so romantic and tragic that it is no wonder that she is still remembered in the village where she once lived. But there are other reasons why they still speak of her in the Bell inn at Thorpe-le-Soken, for although the beautiful Kitty was buried with great ceremony in the church vault in 1752, that was not the last the village was to hear of her.

Catherine (known as Kitty) was born in 1720 to Robert and Judith Canham of Beaumont Hall, a much cherished daughter as other children born into the family unfortunately died young. As she grew older, her beauty attracted admirers, including the Rev Alexander Henry Gough, the vicar of Thorpe, who had soon lost his heart to pretty Kitty, and despite his brother's advice that 'she is a beautiful creature who will play you a trick', he asked for her hand in marriage and was accepted.

The Rev Gough must have sometimes ruefully remembered his brother's warning, as Kitty soon became bored with her life as the vicar's wife and one day gossip spread like wildfire round the village. Mrs Gough had vanished! Tongues wagged and many were the theories about her sudden disappearance. One explanation put forward was that she had gone to London to consult a doctor, and had not returned. The other more exciting rumour had it that she had been seen leaving a masquerade, presumably in London, with a mysterious partner.

Naturally this was the most popular version, and it may have been quite near to the truth as it transpired much later that at some social occasion Kitty had met a charming and well-connected young man, Lord Dalmeny, who fell passionately in love with her and asked her to marry him.

Faced with the choice of marriage to a wealthy young aristocrat or a return to village life as a vicar's wife, beautiful Kitty didn't hesitate. Lord Dalmeny knew nothing of her background and seemingly cared less, so believing her to be a single girl, he and Kitty were married. During the next four years they travelled on the Continent, enjoying a luxurious lifestyle, but Kitty had never been strong, and in 1752 she became seriously ill.

Sadly it was soon clear that there was no hope of recovery and, realising that the moment of truth had arrived, Kitty asked for pen and paper, and managed to write: 'I am the wife of the Reverend Alexander Gough, Vicar of Thorpe le Soken in Essex. My maiden name was Catherine Canham. My last request is to be buried at Thorpe.'

The effect of this bombshell on Lord Dalmeny is not hard to imagine. It was a complete shock to him, but as he held his dying wife in his arms, his love was such that he forgave her deceit and promised to fulfil her last wishes.

Kitty's body was embalmed and encased in an elaborate coffin decorated with large silver plates. The coffin was enclosed in a plain wooden chest, her clothes and jewellery were packed up and her grieving husband left Italy for France. There, adopting the pseudonym of Mr Williams, he set sail for Dover, where he then boarded another ship, bound for Harwich.

But there was rough weather ahead, and the boat was driven into the mouth of the river Colne, where customs officers boarded it and at the sight of the large wooden chest suspected contraband. One of the officers was about to plunge his cutlass into the box but 'Mr Williams' drew his own sword to deter him and told them that the coffin contained the body of his wife. Still unconvinced the customs men opened the coffin and found Kitty's body but they were now inclined to suspect foul play. Dalmeny then admitted that he was not Mr Williams of Hamburg, but a person of quality, and was travelling back from Verona to bring his English wife home for burial.

The customs men were still suspicious that a murder could have been committed, and they placed the coffin in the vestry of Hythe church until the body could be identified. Lord Dalmeny was kept prisoner there too, and he sat beside Kitty's coffin for several days until, among various people who came to look at this unhappy scene, a gentleman arrived who had known Kitty Canham and who recognised the body.

Dalmeny explained to this gentleman that he was the Earl of Rosebery's son, born and educated in Italy, and that he was trying to fulfil his wife's dying wish to be returned to Thorpe for burial.

The *General Evening Post* of 15th August 1752 reported that the Rev Gough was then summoned to Hythe to identify Kitty, and although his first reaction on meeting the man his wife had bigamously married was to threaten to run Lord Dalmeny through with his sword, when they stood there in the presence of the dead woman they had both loved, it was an emotional occasion. And when Dalmeny said that his 'affection for the lady was so strong that it was his earnest wish not only to attend her to the grave, but to be shut up for ever with her there', the two men were united in mutual sympathy and sorrow.

At Kitty's funeral the two husbands, in deep mourning, followed the magnificent hearse hand in hand to her burial in the church vault. Her heartbroken Dalmeny did not linger long after his beloved. He died three years later aged only 31, but the Rev Gough survived for another 22 years.

The Bell overlooks the graveyard at the back, and for

many years it has been assumed that the female ghost who haunts the inn is Kitty. Over the mantelpiece in the bar is a 1960s portrait of a lady with dark hair and eyes, and a wistful expression. She wears an off the shoulder dress with a rose at her bosom and, as I suspected, the landlady told me with warm affection 'That's Kitty'.

There are many stories of Kitty's doings at the pub. Once a shadowy female figure was seen to glide through a closed door, for example, wardrobes have been moved and bedclothes disarranged.

When I visited the Bell in 1994 the landlady told me that 'little things happen, nothing bad' then went on to relate that a few days earlier she had been tidying up a bedroom after some guests had left when she felt really strange. There was a pair of shoes on the floor and as she moved to pick them up, the toe of one tipped right up off the floor as if it was dancing! 'That's the room where things are supposed to happen,' she said, 'It was quite scary for a moment.'

I was able to visit the Bell again recently. They now have two rottweiler dogs and I was told that they will never go into the room they call Kitty's room. The barmaid told me that only the previous week a wardrobe was found moved right away from the wall and no one could imagine how it happened.

'Also,' she went on, 'yesterday there was a quiche on the kitchen table, and suddenly it shot right across the table and onto the floor as I watched, and there was no one else there.' She laughed, 'We always say that's Kitty about again. But there's always a friendly atmosphere. Never anything nasty.'

I believe her. It's a pleasant, cosy pub with old carved beams, a splendid array of horse brasses, and a wooden board on the wall with a list of all the landlords at the Bell dating back to the first, William Shurlock, in 1607. Since I was there previously they had hung a frame over the fireplace enclosing 'Extract from a letter from Colchester dated Aug. 18th 1752', an interesting contemporary account of Kitty's story. I was told that a Dutch lady had brought it in not long ago, explaining that she had found it in her attic!

It may be around 250 years since this 18th-century femme fatale came home to Thorpe-le-Soken but it will be a long time before they forget Kitty, their beautiful bigamist.

The Devil on Wallasea Island

I LOOKED across the bleak expanse of Wallasea Island one dismal day recently and wondered where it had stood, that haunted old edifice they called the Devil's House. It is long gone now, swept away in the great tidal flood of 1953, and perhaps its demons and devils went too as the sea water swept over the whole of Wallasea Island.

The Devil's House was officially known as Tile Barn, a farmhouse with an enormous barn which was reputed to be haunted by either the Devil or some kind of terrifying demon. People recalled that sometimes the cattle in the stockyard seemed to go mad and at these times it was said that the Devil was there, stirring up the animals with his fork! Indeed once in 1938 a herd of cattle charged the stockyard gates and stampeded out over the marsh as if the Devil was after them.

At one time the farm was occupied by Mother Redcap, a notorious local witch whose real name was Granny Smith, and in his book *Ghosts and Witches* James Wentworth Day reported a conversation he had with an old labourer who had worked there. He said that a mate of his found himself thrown out of bed and hauled downstairs one night while they were staying at the farm, and he had no idea how it had happened.

'That old devil were strong as a horse,' was his comment.

The same man had another strange experience one night as he was rowing across the creek from Foulness Island.

Coming over the water in the moonlight he saw Mother Redcap riding along on a wooden hurdle. 'She didn't have no oars, but she travelled same as if she was in a boat,' he said.

A woman whose family occupied the farm when she was a child never forgot her own experience there. She was playing one day in a room with a very high ceiling and noticed that it was becoming icy cold, which was strange as it was a warm summer's day. Then she heard a sound like wings beating high up in the ceiling, which frightened her so she ran to tell her mother, but when they returned the sound had stopped.

She was playing there again the next day, and before long the same icy chill came over the room and again she heard a sound like the movement of huge wings flapping high up in the room. They seemed to be moving slowly at first then gradually beating more and more quickly causing a strong current of cold air. Terrified she called for her mother, and this time her mother too heard the uncanny noise, and after that the room was kept locked.

But some time later when the house was fully occupied at harvest time, a married sister and her baby came to stay and there was only one vacant room available, the former playroom. Knowing nothing of the previous happenings, she went there to sleep, but later emerged terrified. She had woken to find the room becoming not only bitterly cold, but with a terrifying sense of evil, and when she too heard the sound of huge wings beating high up in the air she rushed from the room in a panic.

The farmer investigated, intent on finding some rational explanation. He examined the chimney which seemed perfectly normal, and there was no sign of any hidden area behind the walls. But as he worked he too was conscious of increasing cold and a mounting sensation of fear that made him get out in a hurry and once again the room was locked up and kept closed.

No one used the room again until the First World War, when some soldiers were put up at the farm. They slept in the old barn but their sergeant asked for a room in the house. There was only one available room, the one they kept locked, and without saying too much about it the family tried to discourage him from sleeping there. But the sergeant wouldn't be put off. However, next morning he was found sleeping on the floor outside the room. He looked pale and refused his breakfast and made some excuse about the bed being too soft!

There were always stories about the Devil's House in the Wallasea area. Some said the place was haunted by old Mother Redcap's familiar, and others swore they had seen the Devil himself looking out of the window of the haunted room, horns and all!

One particularly sinister tale concerned a farm labourer who was passing the barn one day when he heard someone call his name. He went inside but there seemed to be nobody about. Then he suddenly began to feel strange and, as if in a dream, he picked up a length of rope and tied it round his neck. A voice was whispering 'Do it, do it,' and he felt an irresistible urge to hang himself. He looked up, ready to throw the end of the rope over a beam, and there looking down at him was a creature out of a nightmare. It was black with gleaming yellow eyes and looked something like an ape. The shock brought him back to normal and he threw down the rope and fled for his life.

When Eric Maple was researching witchcraft in Essex he discovered that a long time ago the house was called Davill's House after the owner, a man called Davill. A cynic might say look no further, obviously the name had been corrupted by superstitious and gullible people into the Devil's House. But further research revealed that although a Frenchman called Daville had owned the house at the time of Charles II, even then it was known as the Devil's Tenement.

No doubt the old tales about this mysterious old farmhouse on Wallasea Island lost nothing in the telling and, anyway, the flood swept it away long ago. Yet stories persist that the Devil has been seen on Wallasea Marshes. And on wild winter nights when the moon gleams on the water and the wind howls across the island like a banshee, who could say for certain that they are wrong?

Haunted Pub Crawl

What Happened to Spider?

NOT many ghosts have a fan club dedicated to them, but at the Bear Inn at Stock the members of the exclusive Spider Club get together once a year for a celebration in honour of Charlie (Spider) Marshall, who will never be forgotten at the ancient hostelry where he used to be the ostler at the turn of the century.

A small man with a curious crab-like gait, Spider had no home or family and lived in the stables at the Bear, where for a free pint or a few coppers he could always be persuaded to perform his trick. Like a shot he would be off, scrambling up the chimney of the taproom fireplace, then reappearing covered in soot down the chimney of the bar parlour.

Sometimes, just to add to the interest, Spider did not immediately reappear. Somewhere where the two chimneys joined was an area, probably a bacon loft, where Spider would hide himself, deaf to all entreaties until the locals would light a bunch of straw and smoke him out.

But Spider tried this trick once too often. One Christmas Eve he refused to budge, and a few high-spirited customers set fire to a bunch of faggots to force him to come down. But even this didn't work, in fact, Spider never did come down at all, and very likely suffocated up there.

Apparently when the bar was altered years later the builders located a small chamber high up in the chimney, thought to be a bacon loft or priest's hole, but when they pushed a long pole in to test its depth, a huge crack devel-

HAUNTED PUB CRAWL

oped in the back of the chimney stack in the centre of the
building. Alarmed that part of the building might collapse,
the crack was quickly cemented over and there were no
more attempts to investigate Spider's hidey-hole.

'If Spider's up there, he can stop there,' said a local
customer. 'They always said the little chap mustn't be
disturbed or he would have his revenge.'

Even so, they say his ghost has been seen 'dodging about
in his boots and white breeches', a tiny figure with an
unmistakable sideways walk. As James Wentworth Day once
wrote, 'Spider has gone but in many ways is still with us.
The most enduring legend of all the inns of Essex. Spider is
immortal.'

The Martyr of Brentwood

IN Brentwood there is a memorial to the local Protestant
martyr, 19 year old William Hunter, a silk weaver's
apprentice, burnt to death in 1555 for his religious beliefs.
It bears the words 'He being dead yet speaketh' which is
oddly apt as a ghost locally believed to be Hunter, although
not actually vocal, has been a restless presence at the inn
where he is said to have spent his last night.

The Swan Hotel in the High Street was originally called
the Argent and later the Gun, becoming the Swan in 1783.
On the night before his death, Hunter had a prophetic
dream in which he was given the chance to recant and save
his life, but he refused.

Events next morning were just as he had dreamed, and as
he was chained to the stake he cried 'Son of God, shine on
me', at which the sun shone out from a dark cloud full on
William's face, to the wonder of the onlookers, and immediately the brushwood and faggots were lit and he was lost to
view in the smoke and flames.

Since then, his ghost has frequently visited the Swan.
One landlady described sudden drops in temperature, the

feeling of a cold presence and noises in the cellar. Furniture has been moved and lights switched on and off, and when the ghost is around dogs react nervously and one used to howl mournfully. Plates hanging on the walls have been thrown down, and police have been called when the outer doors have been found unlocked. And once a clock in an empty room started to strike, and went on striking until it was removed from the wall, although the striking mechanism had not been working for months. There has been the usual ghostly trickery with the beer taps and things disappear and reappear in odd places.

Such poltergeist activity seems a strange manifestation for the ghost of such a high-minded young man as William Hunter must have been. Perhaps the inhabitants at the Swan have been mistaken all along and their ghost is not William at all?

Trouble at the Angel Inn

THERE is nothing like building work and alterations to activate supernatural happenings, and as most new landlords like to make changes when they acquire a pub, frequently they find that they have also acquired a ghost.

This happened in 1962 when Len Brookfield arrived at the Angel Inn in Braintree. Changing the inn sign may not seem too drastic, but Mr Brookfield thought that instead of the more conventional picture of an angel, he would commemorate the day in the last war when the pub had a narrow escape from a Luftwaffe bomb. So the new sign showed an angel riding astride a bomb as she merrily knocked back a pint.

This did not go down at all well with some locals who said the 'angel' was more like a witch and it was all in very bad taste. And when it soon appeared that the pub was now haunted, people remembered that a former landlord's dying wish was that his beloved pub should never be altered. It looked as if his ghost had come back to express his disapproval.

Mr Brookfield had three large guard dogs, two boxers and a collie, who were well aware of the ghost – and terrified. Night after night their howling would wake the landlord who went down to find them, hair on end, shaking with fright. 'When the dogs wake me I find that doors I've closed are open, bottles and glasses have been moved and lights are switched on again,' he said.

Years later, a different landlord started to build an extension at the back and one day a pile of plasterboard was leaning against the bar and, with no one near it, it suddenly crashed to the ground as if it had been pushed over.

Another family who took over the Angel in the 1980s heard 'invisible people' walking about and talking in the night, and once saw a shadowy figure come down the stairs. And the landlord's son once witnessed an ashtray flying off the bar by itself.

However, after the inn sign was altered to show a 'proper angel' the paranormal activity quietened down, so perhaps that old landlord is happy now – at least until someone else takes over the pub and decides to make a few changes!

The Golden Fleece, Brentwood

THIS ancient hostelry is believed to stand on the site of the 12th-century priory of St Peter, which may account for the apparitions of monks that have been seen there from time to time.

It used to be a changing point for horses on the London to Harwich stage run, and one VIP said to have stayed there en route for Harwich was Lord Nelson.

One woman guest staying at the inn had a particularly chilling experience. She was looking in her bedroom mirror when in the glass she suddenly saw, behind her, the figure of a monk standing with his arms folded. She turned round to face the intruder, but there was no one there, yet when she looked back in the mirror the monk was still reflected there.

Besides occasional sightings of ghostly monks, there have been movements of pots and pans in the kitchen and glasses in the bar.

The Black Horse, White Roding

THE lanes around this delightful old gabled pub were full of primroses and violets when I called recently in springtime. Inside it is small and cosy with low beams shining with rows of horse brasses, and walls decorated with brass plaques and nice old pictures. It has an inn sign I would like to frame for my own wall, showing a top hatted gentleman with his splendid black horse, reminiscent of a Stubbs painting.

Despite its charm and comfort, the Black Horse has a long history of haunting. In 1984 two customers watched an old man with a stick hobble into the bar only to vanish in front of them! In the nineties there were all kinds of nocturnal noises coming from the bar and cellar, and once a foot high crystal ornament fell down from a height and landed without breaking. And from time to time glasses used to slide along the bar.

Alan Harris took over the pub in 1995 and soon found that although the lights were all switched off at night, he would come down in the morning to find them on. At first he and his wife accused each other of forgetting to turn them off, but they soon realised it was one of the resident ghost's little tricks.

When they were moving in they were puzzled to notice that the gable at the end of the building had two windows outside, but only one inside. The answer was that a lower ceiling had been put in over part of the bar to block off the high roof as it was so cold, and this area which included the second window was walled off upstairs. The only entrance was a small trapdoor in the corner of the bar. However, one night after going outside to say goodbye to some friends, Mr and Mrs Harris noticed that there was a light on up there. But there is no electricity or other lighting!

'Did you go up?' I asked Mr Harris.

He laughed. 'I just poked my head through the trap door,' he said, 'but all I saw were the water tanks.'

Not long ago a couple stayed for B & B, and at breakfast they asked who was playing the piano in the night. There is no piano in the pub, but later Mr Harris was told that there once was a piano and the ghost used to play it after hours! So apparently he still manages to give the occasional recital, piano or no piano.

The Oldest Inn in England

I MUST confess to a feeling of surprise when I first saw St Anne's Castle at Great Leighs, it certainly did not live up to my idea of the oldest licensed public house in England. But it transpires that the front was once badly damaged by fire and had to be rebuilt. It was formerly a hermitage known as Saint Anne's, according to *White's Gazetteer of Essex*, where pilgrims en route to Thomas à Becket's shrine used to stay.

The inn has had a reputation for being haunted for as long as anyone can remember and appears to have two separate stories to account for the happenings. It has a haunted room upstairs, where there used to be a four poster bed which nearly filled the room, and one story is that a child was murdered there in the presence of the mother long ago, so long ago in fact that no details of what happened remain.

In 1939 the 14 year old daughter of the landlord slept in this room and was terrified by a presence. She felt cold and clammy and could see a figure standing at the bottom of her bed which vanished when she screamed. She moved to another bedroom, taking her dog with her for company, but the dog obviously sensed the atmosphere upstairs and would growl at something unseen.

After the haunting at St Anne's Castle inn was featured on the BBC in April 1939, many would-be ghosthunters wanted to stay in the haunted bedroom. Several people reported waking to see a black shape in the room, loud cries have been heard, also various bangs and raps, cold draughts and sometimes the curtains were pulled down and the bedclothes ripped off the bed.

The second instalment of the haunting at the inn came during the last war. Not far away is Scrapfaggot Green, a small triangle of grass where three roads join. Scrapfaggot is a local name for a witch, and on this small patch of ground the body of a witch was reputed to be buried, with a huge boulder on top of her grave to prevent her ghost from straying, a pious hope that was to be frustrated.

During the war it's said that American military trucks on their way to the airfield had difficulty getting round Scrapfaggot Green and the enormous stone, so they bulldozed it flat to enable them to drive straight across more easily, and in doing so they uncovered the witch's ancient grave. Her bones and the charred remains of her funeral pyre were exposed and what happened then has never been forgotten in the village.

The clock on the parish church began to go backwards, the church bell chimed of its own accord, haystacks collapsed mysteriously and overnight one farmer's hens were exchanged for another farmer's ducks! Worse than that, all kinds of alarming things began to happen at the pub so that local people believed that the spirit of the witch, now released, had taken up residence there.

In the landlord's bedroom it was complete mayhem. Furniture was overturned and clothes and bedding strewn all over the floor, and however often the room was put right it all happened again, although from downstairs no sound had been heard. A drayman delivering beer one day shot out of the cellar and stood shaking beside his dray, insisting that he would never go down into the cellar again. 'Not after that thing was standing behind me,' he said and that was the last they saw of him.

And a young girl in the pub with her friend suddenly gave a piercing scream and cried, 'Look at that thing in the fireplace.' And fainted dead away. No one else could see anything and when the girl came round she said she had seen a frightening shape like a human figure standing in the large fireplace.

When I called at the pub a framed press cutting on the wall said that in 1982 a barmaid saw the ghost of a Victorian lady, and mentions flying cutlery, falling pictures and sightings of a grey lady and a black witch.

The inn is still a target for psychic investigators, but when I last visited, the fairly new landlord told me that nothing had happened since he had been there. And the famous four poster bed has now gone. One psychic investigation team spent several hours in the pub one night in the summer of 1996, but after setting up their cameras, thermo-meters, tape recorders and so on, and stationing members at strategic points throughout the pub and cellar, no paranormal activity rewarded their vigil.

Have the ghosts all left Essex's most famous haunted inn? Time will tell. It's said that one in five of all Essex pubs are, or were, haunted and these are just a few of the county's inns with an interesting ghost story to tell.

Index

111